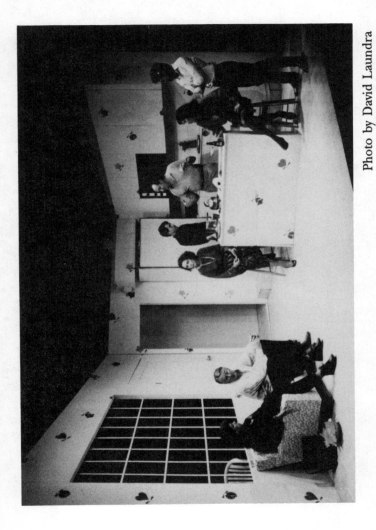

A scene from the Perry Street Theater production of "Carbondale Dreams." Set design by Jeff Freund.

CARBONDALE DREAMS

BY STEVEN SATER

DRAMATISTS
PLAY SERVICE
INC.

SPECIAL NOTE ON
SONGS AND RECORDINGS

For performance of such songs and recordings mentioned in this play as are in copyright, the permission of the copyright owners must be obtained; or other songs and recordings in the public domain substituted.

2

SPECIAL MUSIC NOTE

SPECIAL MUSIC TAPE

A cassette tape containing the original music composed by Patricia Lee Stotter for the New York Production of this play is available through the Play Service at $20.00 per tape. A cue sheet is included with the tape. There is additional royalty of $10.00 per performance for the use of this music by producing groups.

SOUND EFFECTS

An audio cassette tape containing the sound effects which may be used in connection with the production of this play, may be obtained from Thomas J. Valentino, Inc., 151 West 46th Street, New York, N.Y. 10036.

Telephone ring
Car horn
Doorbell (extended ring)
Doorbell (singular ring)

3

This play is dedicated to my brother, my sister, my father and my mother. With deep appreciation to Daisaku Ikeda. And special thanks to Jeff, Cheryl, Byam, Ginger, Carol, and my beloved wife Lori.

CARBONDALE DREAMS first opened under the title BRADLEY AND BETH, off-off Broadway at the Perry Street Theater (Lion King Productions in association with The Writers Theatre), in New York City on October 12th, 1989. It was directed by Byam Stevens; the set design was by Jeff Freund; the costume design was by Rosi Zingales; the lighting design was by Stan Pressner; the music was by Patricia Lee Stotter; and the production stage manager was Jennifer Gilbert. The cast was as follows:

ARNOLD	Robert Trumbull
BARONE	Anita Keal
BETH	Navida Stein
DAVID	James Lish
BARRY	James Maxson
BETTY	Heather Coleman
BRADLEY	Jeff Bender
CANDI	Cheryl Thornton
BRIAN	J.R. Nutt

In November, 1989, the play moved off-Broadway to the Judith Anderson Theater (Lion King Productions), where its title became CARBONDALE DREAMS. There was one cast change: Deanna DuClos replaced Heather Coleman as BETTY. The character BRIAN was removed from the play.

ARNOLD joined the other two plays of CARBONDALE DREAMS on December 26, 1989. The cast was as follows:

ARNOLD	Richard Thomsen
BARONE	Anita Keal

CARBONDALE DREAMS transferred to the Kaufman Theater (Lion King Productions in association with Martin R. Kaufman) on January 26, 1990. It was directed by Rand Foerster; the set design was by Jeff Freund; the costume design was by Rosi Zingales; the lighting design was by Steve Shelley; the music was by Patricia Lee Stotter; and the production stage manager was Sean P. Reilly. The cast was as follows:

ARNOLD ....Richard Thomsen
BARONE ....Anita Keal
BETH ....Navida Stein
DAVID ....James Lish
BARRY...Bob Ari
BETTY ....Deanna DuClos
BRADLEY...Jeff Bender
CANDI ....Cheryl Thornton

During the run at the Kaufman Theater, the cast changes were as follows: George Axler took over the role of ARNOLD; Lois Markle took over the role of BARONE; Harry S. Murphy took over the role of BARRY; Richard Topol took over the role of DAVID; and Jennifer Ann Kelly took over the role of BETTY.

CHARACTERS

ARNOLD — Mid to late 50's. Grey, wiry, born in Carbondale.

BARONE — Arnold's wife. One year younger. A beautiful Jewish girl from Dallas. (She speaks with no accent.)

BETH — Mid 30's. The princess grown up, overweight.

DAVID — Beth's brother, a bit younger. The poet who moved to New York.

BARRY — Beth's husband, late 30's. The "right kind of boy" to have married.

BETTY — Beth's daughter, age 6-8. Loves Mommy.

BRADLEY — Beth and David's brother. About 30. The renegade son grown up.

CANDI — Bradley's college sweetheart, now his wife. Born in Kentucky, bone-thin.

TIME AND PLACE

Act I ~ Arnold — The living room of Barone and Arnold's home in Carbondale, Illinois. One afternoon, just before Thanksgiving.

Act II ~ Beth — The kitchen of Beth's home, set beside a lake on the outskirts of Carbondale, Illinois. Later that afternoon, just before Thanksgiving.

Act III ~ Bradley — The last empty room in Bradley and Candi's new home in Carbondale, Illinois. Late that same evening, just before Thanksgiving.

AUTHOR'S NOTE

From the very beginning I conceived the plays of *Carbondale Dreams* as plays that could be performed separately or together. All together, they tell one story, the incidents of one evening; individually, each tells one character's story. Each is a myth of one member of this family.

Bradley was written first and plays last. It began as a reading at the Actors Studio, and I owe a great debt of gratitude to Jeff Bender and Cheryl Thornton for the years we met and read the script aloud in my apartment as I reworked it. I also owe a great debt to Byam Stevens for his dramaturgical work on this and on the two other acts of this play. Throughout the script the characters' lines end with three dots. It is not that their thoughts are left incomplete, but perhaps that thought itself is incomplete for the feeling each possesses of what is beyond him. The dots really indicate pauses. The actors should not provide further words after the dots, as if their characters knew what they were going to say but got cut off. I set the play on the floor, but in New York David always sat on a stereo speaker and sometimes Bradley did. The play seems to have the most dramatic impact when played for its full humor.

Beth came next. In our New York production many speeches overlapped. Two or three conversations would go on at once, and of course many particular lines were lost. (I have put brackets in the left-hand margin of this text where we overlapped the lines. Often the lines just before or just after this overlap would act almost as a punch line; and certain lines within the overlap would jump out: e.g., Barone's "I must have done something right as a Mother." But another production might discover other options. The principles for the overlapping are simple: see who is talking to whom and allow the conversation between one pair to go on uninterrupted at the same time as the conversation of another pair.) There are a few places where this must happen — i.e., when Beth talks to Candi on the phone and Barone pulls aside David, but there are other times when the lines might be allowed to fall in sequence without any overlap whatsoever: a more stylized way of presenting all the simultaneous talking. In any case, the heightened riot begins to depict what is inside Beth, so the buildup of voice and volume leads to her explosion.

Arnold written last, plays first. In fact in New York we often performed **Beth** and **Bradley** only, and sometimes **Arnold** and **Beth**, and sometimes all three. **Arnold** too must be allowed its humor. When the emptiness beneath the talk is played for tragic impact, the playing gets too slow and seems pretentious. Or so I feel. Still it is a gentle play, whose subject is a silence.

For months we performed *Carbondale Dreams* on relatively traditional sets on a proscenium arch. The flats folded back to become this house or that house. But also for months we did the show with little or no set, in a house with audience on two sides; and both ways seemed to work. **Beth** does require some kitchen stuff; **Arnold** needs a table; **Bradley** needs at least a representation of some carpet; but that's it. The plays play fast and best without too many beats or pauses that aren't scripted.

When I wrote these plays I provided no stage directions and almost no comment on any of the characters' intentions. In this script I filled in many notes of what we discovered during the run in New York: e.g., the dimmings up and down of the lights during **Bradley,** David's comic gesture to quiet Beth after her explosion. Please feel free to ignore any of them. Like the overlapping these notes are offered only as suggestions.

Finally, I'm enclosing here a prologue, epilogue, and two entr'acte speeches for David. I wrote them to provide a sense of completeness to the evening, though perhaps the plays really don't need them. (We never performed them in New York, but by the time I'd completed them we were no longer doing **Arnold.**) They do introduce each act in a humorous way; and they do present a different side of David.

9

			01 02:50
Apr-29 02:54:20	678		CI-INDY-FS/SY
			has been chan
			01 02:45
Apr-29 02:54:20	678		CI-INDY-FS/SY
			has been chan
			01 02:50
Apr-29 02:54:20	678		CI-INDY-FS/SY
			has been chan
			01 02:45
Apr-29 02:54:20	678		CI-INDY-FS/SY
			has been chan
			01 02:50
Apr-29 02:54:20	678		CI-INDY-FS/SY
			has been chan
			01 02:45
Apr-29 02:54:20	678		CI-INDY-FS/SY
			has been chan
			01 02:50
Apr-29 02:54:20	678		CI-INDY-FS/SY
			has been chan
			01 02:45
Apr-29 02:54:20	678		CI-INDY-FS/SY
			has been chan
			01 02:50
Apr-29 02:54:20	678		CI-INDY-FS/SY
			timestamp has
			to Apr 29 01
Apr-29 02:54:20	678		CI-INDY-FS/SY
			timestamp has
			to Apr 29 01

CARBONDALE DREAMS

PROLOGUE

David stands alone Onstage, spotlit.

DAVID. So I got this call from my Mother, right? Really. *(A beat. He speaks as his Mother.)* "Honey, don't come home for Thanksgiving." *(Now as himself.)* "What?" *(Now as his Mother.)* "Honey, don't come home. Don't come home to see *me*. So what if I die without seeing you? What's the big thing?" *(A beat.)* "Honey, don't come home to see your brother Bradley. God help him, David. Your talking won't change anything." *(A beat.)* "Baby, don't come home to see Beth, your poor sister. Oh, David, it goes beyond decency! You know I've tried everything. What is there left that another human being could say?" *(A beat.)* "David, don't come home to see your poor father. My husband! Who knew he'd turn out this way?" *(A beat.)* "No, David, come home so *you* can be happy." *(A beat. Now he speaks as himself.)* "But, Mom, if I want to be happy I'll stay here, okay?" *(A beat.)* And I slammed down the phone. An adult now; defiant. *(A beat.)* The next day I called up and booked my seat on the plane. *(A beat.)* I called my Mother. She said, "Oh, I'm so happy. Now I can go to my grave without being in pain." *(A beat.)*

BLACKOUT

11

ARNOLD

ACT I

*Music at the top. As music ends, lights come up on Arnold
alone Onstage, swinging a golf club. Swings again. Is unable
to complete his swing as he wishes.*

ARNOLD.   Damn. *(Tries again, and fails.)* Dammit. *(Calling off.)*
Barone. *(No response.)* Barone.
BARONE.   *(Offstage. Calling back.)* What is it?
ARNOLD.   Barone, what time is David coming in?
BARONE.   At five o'clock, honey. You know, that five o'clock
plane.
ARNOLD.   That five o'clock plane?
BARONE.   You know the one. That flight that sets down in
Dayton. You just sit down, and have time to get up and go to
the bathroom, and then all the people are piling on again.
You know the one.
ARNOLD.   From Dayton.
BARONE.   The one where I always ask you to get me a 7-Up.
ARNOLD.   I know the one. *(As he settles back to the club.)*
BARONE.   Honey. *(No answer. He begins swinging his golf club
again.)* Honey.
ARNOLD.   What, honey?
BARONE.   Honey, do you think we should call Bradley?
ARNOLD.   Call Bradley? Why, honey?
BARONE.   To make sure he picks David up.
ARNOLD.   Honey, the boy is thirty-two years old.
BARONE.   He's still our son. Don't you know our son? Maybe
I'll just call Candi to see if he's left for the airport or not.
ARNOLD.   Honey, you know what's going to happen when

12

you do that.

BARONE. When I do what?

ARNOLD. When you call Candi to ask if Brad's left or not. You know how she's going to take that.

BARONE. Do you expect me, Arnie, to live my life like that, around what Candi wants? I just can't live my life like that, Arnie: scurrying around the bike track of what Candi wants. I've lived my life like that with you for too long. *(A beat as Arnold swings his club.)* Honey, I'm calling her up. *(Silence. While Arnold is swinging his golf club, we hear Barone dialing, then speaking from offstage.)* Arnie —

ARNOLD. *(Breaking swing.)* What is it? Damn it.

BARONE. Arnie, I've got that damn answering machine. Do you think I should hang up?

ARNOLD. What?

BARONE. *(Now speaking into machine.)* Candi, this is Mom. I mean, Barone. I'm just calling to make sure Brad's up and off to pick his brother up. We look forward to seeing you and your kids so much. Forgive me, I'm a mother. I was calling my son. *(She hangs up. Calls back in.)* Honey, I left a message.

ARNOLD. Okay, Barone.

BARONE. Okay what?

ARNOLD. Just okay, Barone. So you left a message.

BARONE. What?

ARNOLD. Nothing.

BARONE. What?

ARNOLD. Nothing. I'm sure they've both gone to pick Dave up.

BARONE. Arnie, don't you know your son? *(Arnold swings his golf club, hard.)* I knew you should have been the one to go pick him up. *(Pause. Barone enters, in bathrobe. Carrying two dresses. She looks at Arnold. Then crosses close to him, holding a magenta, or deep pink silk dress up in front of herself.)* Honey, do you like this color?

ARNOLD. *(Who'd been absorbed, reacts as if shocked.)* What?

BARONE. Honey, I'm sorry. I didn't mean to interrupt the episode with the club.

ARNOLD. What is it, Barone?

13

BARONE. It was nothing. Forget it.

ARNOLD. What was it?

BARONE. I just wanted to know, but forget it, whether or not you liked this color, or not.

ARNOLD. Which color?

BARONE. This pink.

ARNOLD. The hot pink.

BARONE. It's not hot. I mean, it isn't really hot. I mean, I just thought David might like to see his old mom in her high-fashion style. I mean, of course, it's not like what he can get in New York; what he sees on his designer friends in their macrobiotic spots. But I just thought, maybe, this pink would be good on his mom ...

ARNOLD. I like that pink for his mom.

BARONE. You don't think it's too hot?

ARNOLD. What's hot on a mom?

BARONE. I don't know. I just think, maybe the pink is too hot.

ARNOLD. What are the other choices we have for our son?

BARONE. I don't know. Then there are just those pants from Bonwit's.

ARNOLD. What pants from Bonwit's?

BARONE. Arnie, the pants from Bonwit's.

ARNOLD. Oh, the pants from Bonwit's.

BARONE. Remember them? The blue silk pants I picked up at Bonwit's. Remember that incident? Remember that?

ARNOLD. At Bonwit's?

BARONE. When that woman, the salesgirl at Bonwit's, accused me of stealing my husband's charge card.

ARNOLD. Oh, you mean those blue pants from Bonwit's.

BARONE. That's what I've been saying. The blue pants from Bonwit's.

ARNOLD. How much were those pants?

BARONE. Arnie, this was Bonwit's.

ARNOLD. Silk or something, weren't they, the pants?

BARONE. My blue silk pants from Bonwit's. *(A beat.)*

ARNOLD. I like those pants.

BARONE. Honey, do you think David would like them?

ARNOLD. Now I can't say that.

BARONE. I just never know what he likes any more. I don't see him.

ARNOLD. Call him and ask.

BARONE. Honey, he's already boarded the plane. He'll be landing.

ARNOLD. But this is important.

BARONE. *(After a beat.)* You like the blue jacket?

ARNOLD. Which jacket?

BARONE. The jacket I wore that night with the slacks from Bonwit's.

ARNOLD. I like that jacket.

BARONE. You do?

ARNOLD. Do you wear a pin on that?

BARONE. My diamond from Zeyda.

ARNOLD. Uh huh.

BARONE. Uh huh what?

ARNOLD. Barone, I thought you looked nice when you wore the whole outfit. Barone in her Bonwit's ... I think I said that.

BARONE. I'll never forget it ... That night I wore it to the Kennel Club ...

ARNOLD. Uh huh ...

BARONE. And you just said to me, "Barone, you look nice in that outfit." I'll never forget it. *(A silence.)* Arnie, why did you ask if I wore a pin on that? *(No response.)* Arnie?

ARNOLD. I don't know, dolly. Seems like I remembered some kind of pin on the jacket. *(A beat.)*

BARONE. Oh. *(A beat.)* Oh. *(A beat.)* Was that all?

ARNOLD. What?

BARONE. Just something on the jacket. *(A beat.)* Something on the jacket ... *(A silence.)* Could have been an insect, or a lint ball ... Just a something on the jacket. *(A beat.)* Arnie, there was never an insect on my jacket.

ARNOLD. I know that. *(A beat. Barone sighs. Then:)*

BARONE. Someday I've got to find out how it is I got here ... *(A beat.)* Trapped in this Carbondale life with my mouth here talking ... *(A beat, Barone begins to exit.)*

ARNOLD. *(As she's going.)* What time does his flight get in?

BARONE. I told you, five o'clock. *(A pause.)* I'm going now, Arnie ... *(A beat.)* Going back to my room now to try on the blue slacks ...

ARNOLD. Alone, or with the jacket?

BARONE. Well, I don't know. I mean, what would you say if I just bopped in in the jacket? *(A beat.)* Arnie, if I just wear in the new blue jacket, will you take a look at it? *(A pause.)* Arnie ...

ARNOLD. All right. *(He doesn't budge. Swings the golf club. A beat.)*

BARONE. Now he's back to the club, and I'm left with his "all right." *(A beat.)* All right ... *(A pause.)* Arnie, I'll try on the jacket a'nd see if you think David would like it. *(She exits with the two dresses. He swings the golf club. A moment or two of silence, Arnold swinging the golf club. He realigns his stance, shifts his feet and ... from offstage:)* Arnie —

ARNOLD. What is it?

BARONE. Arnie —

ARNOLD. What is it?

BARONE. Arnie, I'm standing here looking at this outfit.

ARNOLD. Which outfit?

BARONE. Arnie, my blue slacks from Bonwit's.

ARNOLD. I like the slacks.

BARONE. Arnie, you don't think the slacks are too tight? *(No response.)* I know you were thinking "Barone's gotten fat ..." *(A beat.)* It's my thyroid, Arnie. You know that. Once you start taking pills to make thyroid, how can you ever tell if your life's in your own hands? *(A beat.)* I mean, what is it but death to keep chasing your body? What are you chasing, with the hours on the bike; the golf swings; and now, aerobic walking ...? I mean, you can't cure cancer by exercise. *(A beat. Barone enters, in blue jacket and slacks.)* Okay. Here it is, Arnie. *(No response.)* Arnie. *(No response.)* Arnie, here's the blue jacket and slacks from Bonwit's. *(No response.)* Arnie ...

ARNOLD. All right with the Bonwit's. *(A beat.)*

BARONE. You promised, Arnie.

ARNOLD. All right, Barone. All right. *(He looks up from golf swing, stands, judging her outfit, a beat, then.)* Barone, I like it.

BARONE. You like it? You think David would like it?

ARNOLD. I think I like it, Barone.

BARONE. You do?

ARNOLD. *(After he looks at it, considers.)* On the left side.

BARONE. The left side?

ARNOLD. Let's see the pin on the left side. *(Barone removes pin, moves it to left side. She looks up.)* There now, I like it.

BARONE. You like it on the left side?

ARNOLD. Uh huh.

BARONE. Hold on a minute, Arnie. *(Barone moves Arnold aside, so she can look, from where Arnold was swinging, into mirror. She'll be looking, really, directly out at audience.)* I just want to look in the mirror, and see with you by me if I like it on the left side.

ARNOLD. You asked me what I liked.

BARONE. I did, but I have to see for myself how it looks on the left.

ARNOLD. Okay, I'll buy it.

BARONE. *(Looking in mirror.)* Arnie, the thing is, from here, in the mirror — I mean, you just can't believe it. I just see it on the right side ...

ARNOLD. That's the mirror, Barone. Take my word for it.

BARONE. I'll try it on the right side.

ARNOLD. What?

BARONE. So I can see it on the left.

ARNOLD. Barone ...

BARONE. Just look at us, Arnie. There we are, two souls in our clothes.

ARNOLD. But, Barone, only you are wearing Bonwit's.

BARONE. I know that ... I mean, look how you've aged, Arnie.

ARNOLD. Barone.

BARONE. I mean, who would have dreamed we'd come out like this? I mean, I know I get caught up in pins and blue jackets. I know it's not living from the soul ... But here we are, Arnie. Our David is coming home. And you have to tell him you have leukemia. And I have to sit there alone. Thinking about what you're telling him on your own. I mean, let's just take this one moment to say we are here: this is it; this is home ... You can see it in our reflection, Arnie. You can ...

17

ARNOLD. All right, Barone.

BARONE. Let's just take this moment and remember we're home. *(A pause.)* Then each of us will have it later — a moment out of time ... *(They stand still, a moment. Pause; then.)* How are you doing?

ARNOLD. I'm remembering this.

BARONE. Okay, good.

ARNOLD. Now can we get back to the golf swing?

BARONE. What do you want for food?

ARNOLD. What?

BARONE. For food. *(A beat.)* Arnie, food ... *(A beat.)* You have to eat something before you sit down with your son ... Preferably something good ... Now, I've got cornbread in there that I baked for him. Macrobiotic cornbread.

ARNOLD. That sounds good.

BARONE. How about that with some peanut butter or what?

ARNOLD. How about that, Barone?

BARONE. Arnie, what is it?

ARNOLD. Just give me a kiss, Barone.

BARONE. Do you mean it?

ARNOLD. Uh huh.

BARONE. Well, you start ...

ARNOLD. I like you in those clothes. *(Arnold kisses Barone. A long kiss. An embrace. As he starts to kiss her again ....)*

BARONE. You like me in these clothes?

ARNOLD. *(Moving to kiss her again.)* Oh, I do, Barone.

BARONE. You do?

ARNOLD. I do. *(They kiss.)*

BARONE. Arnie, could you put down the golf club?

ARNOLD. I — no — I don't know.

BARONE. No?

ARNOLD. Honey — well — well, we'll see — uh — after the food.

BARONE. I just thought, maybe, before David gets here, you know ...

ARNOLD. Barone, after the food.

BARONE. Arnie, I've got that cornbread. I think I've got watermelon too.

ARNOLD. I'll bet you do. *(A beat.)*

BARONE. Arnie, can you believe we might — well — uh —

ARNOLD. Barone, after some food. I've just got to get through this swing.

BARONE. Okay, I know. I think I've got that crunchy Deaf Smith.

ARNOLD. Sounds good.

BARONE. And then there's watermelon too ... I'll just go see what else there is.

ARNOLD. Sounds good ...

BARONE. *(One last try, before breaking away.)* Arnie ...

ARNOLD. What?

BARONE. I mean ...

ARNOLD. Barone. I've just got to get through this swing.

BARONE. Okay, I know. *(Breaking apart, gently, from Arnold.)* I'll just try to get you a nice kind of plate of food.

ARNOLD. Our kind of food.

BARONE. "Our kind of food ..." *(She goes off to the kitchen, as if in a dream, wistful, light, and slow ...We hear her singing a Broadway love song of the 1950's like "Till There Was You ..." Then.)* Arnie ... *(No response.)* Arnie ...

ARNOLD. What is it, Barone?

BARONE. Arnie, I've got a little slaw. *(A beat.)* Arnie, would you like a little slaw? *(A beat.)*

ARNOLD. Is that the slaw you made, Barone?

BARONE. Uh huh. *(A beat.)*

ARNOLD. Barone, I'll have a little slaw. *(A beat.)*

BARONE. *(Entering, with a tray of food.)* Okay, here's your peanut butter sandwich. And here's just a little side dish of slaw. *(She sets tray down on table.)* Now you just sit down before it gets too hot.

ARNOLD. What?

BARONE. A joke ... *(Arnold leans golf club against wall. Meanwhile Barone looks at plates. Rearranges watermelon. Then rearranges slaw.)* Honey, what a colorful lunch. *(Arnold comes to table. Sits down. He looks down at plates. Moves plate of slaw to where melon is; moves melon to where slaw was.)* Oh, my God!

ARNOLD. What is it, honey?

BARONE. My God, it's after 4:00 o'clock.

ARNOLD. You said he's coming in at five.

BARONE. But then if you and I wanted to — you know, Arnie ...

ARNOLD. Honey, just let me get settled with the slaw.

BARONE. Okay, hon ... *(A silence.)* Now why don't I try on the hot dress just so we'll both know?

ARNOLD. Can't you just sit with me awhile?

BARONE. I'm flattered. Sure. *(She sits at table, a beat. He eats.)* I've got some of that two-day-old three-bean salad, if you'd like some.

ARNOLD. No thank you.

BARONE. No more slaw. *(A pause, he continues to eat.)* Honey, what time is it?

ARNOLD. Barone, it's after four o'clock.

BARONE. Now, just sit there, one minute. One minute. And let me just run in one minute. One minute. And show you this watermelon-colored dress.

ARNOLD. All right, but, Barone —

BARONE. What? *(A beat.)* We'll still have time ...

ARNOLD. Barone —

BARONE. *(Getting up from table.)* Just give me one second.

ARNOLD. *(A call from his heart.)* Does your outfit really have to mean so much?

BARONE. Well, I don't know.

ARNOLD. I mean, can't you just sit down with me, honey?

BARONE. Arnie —

ARNOLD. Just one minute.

BARONE. I — no — I don't know.

ARNOLD. *(Taking her hand.)* Barone, won't you join me for a bit of watermelon?

BARONE. Arnie, my Davey's coming home. I want to look good. *(Barone exits, to her room. Arnold sits for a moment at the table. As if picking at his food. Draws the watermelon to him. Begins to weep over it. A moment, then: offstage, calling.)* Arnie.

ARNOLD. What is it?

BARONE. I'll just be a moment. *(Arnold pushes the watermelon away from him. A pause.)* Arnie.

ARNOLD. All right, Barone. *(A pause.)*
BARONE. Arnie, I'm coming.
ARNOLD. Okay, good. *(A beat. Barone enters in the pink dress.)*
BARONE. Arnie, here I am.
ARNOLD. *(Still looking away.)* Okay, just a moment.
BARONE. Oh, God, Arnie, here I am.
ARNOLD. *(Turning to her.)* Let's see.
BARONE. It feels so good. *(A beat.)*
ARNOLD. *(The verdict.)* I like it too.
BARONE. More than the blue?
ARNOLD. I like it too.
BARONE. But, Arnie, I've got to choose between this and the blue.
ARNOLD. I guess that's just a decision I can't make for you, Barone. *(A beat.)*
BARONE. This isn't too hot?
ARNOLD. Barone, what's hot in a watermelon outfit?
BARONE. I don't know.
ARNOLD. *(Standing up.)* I do.
BARONE. You do?
ARNOLD. Uh huh ... I like this one best.
BARONE. You do?
ARNOLD. I do. *(A beat, he steps toward Barone.)* I like the way this pretty pink outfit brings out all the life in you. The color in your cheeks ... *(A beat.)* I like the way this goes with your eyes.
BARONE. You do, really? Better than the blue?
ARNOLD. Uh huh.
BARONE. I knew when I put on this outfit you'd like it best. I knew ...
ARNOLD. You see, you knew. *(A beat.)* Will you dance with me, Barone? Will you do that, a minute?
BARONE. Will I do what?!
ARNOLD. Will you dance with me, honey? We can sing Frank Sinatra ... Remember the time we danced in Dad's basement?
BARONE. Arnie, I can't believe you could ask me! *(Arnold takes Barone in his arms, begins to dance with her.)*

21

ARNOLD. *(Sings, as they dance.)* "Heaven, I'm in heaven. And my heart beats so that I can hardly speak ..."
BARONE. *(Joining in with Arnold who still sings.)* "And I seem to find the happiness I seek ..."
"When we're out together dancing cheek to cheek ..." *
(Arnold begins humming next chorus of song, dancing with Barone.)
BARONE. Oh, Arnie ... *(He hums more of song, and they keep dancing.)* Arnie.
ARNOLD. What is it, Barone? *(A beat, as they continue dancing.)*
BARONE. Oh, Arnie, how long has it been since I've been in your arms? *(They dance.)* Oh, Arnie, sing me about heaven ...
ARNOLD. *(Singing, gently.)* "Heaven, I'm in heaven ..." *
BARONE. *(As he sings.)* Oh, Arnie, Arnie, we're home ... *(They dance. Arnold sings; and then hums the song. He embraces Barone, begins to unbutton her dress.)* Oh, my God, Arnie, wait.
ARNOLD. What?
BARONE. What time is it, Arnie?
ARNOLD. What?
BARONE. Arnie, what time is it? I'll bet it's five o'clock.
ARNOLD. So what?
BARONE. What?
ARNOLD. So what, Barone?
BARONE. "So what?"! *(A beat.)* Arnie, I don't know how you can stand there and say to me, "So what".
ARNOLD. So what? So what? So what? So what?
BARONE. Arnie, it's almost five o'clock. *(A beat.)* David's plane is landing at five o'clock.
ARNOLD. Honey, Brad's going to pick David up.
BARONE. Oh, Arnie, for God's sake, don't you know Bradley, your son? *(A beat.)* I mean, I said, when you called him this morning, "Arnie, you should go and pick him up ..." I said, "Arnie, you know you can't trust Bradley. You know he'll never go to pick Dave up ..." *(A beat.)* I want my David to feel comfortable, honey, while he rides through town in your new Mercedes. I want my David to know I made corn-

---

* Used by permission. See Special Music Note on copyright page.

bread. And when he comes home I want my David to see his old Mom in her drop-dead hot pink outfit. I want my David —

ARNOLD. *(Interrupting.)* You want your David to what? *(A beat. A silence. Arnold extricates himself. A moment.)*

BARONE. Arnie, what is it?

ARNOLD. Nothing. Nothing, hon.

BARONE. Huh? *(A beat.)*

ARNOLD. Oh, for God's sake, Barone, enough! Enough! Enough with your talk of your god-damn pink outfit. Enough with your asking "What time is it, Arnie?" Enough, Barone. It's just enough. *(A beat.)* It's been thirty-nine god-damn years of your talking. Can't you just shut up your mouth just one moment? It's sickening, having to stand here and listen. You know, this is what keeps us so damn apart, so damn alone. You're too busy manufactuirng moments to let something beautiful just happen. Damn it, Barone, do you think if I'd had you I'd ever have picked up the golf club? *(A beat.)*

BARONE. I don't know.

ARNOLD. You don't? *(A beat, Barone sighs.)*

BARONE. Oh, no. *(A deep pause. Arnold crosses in fury, in silence, to pick up golf club. Swings it, hard. Another long pause, and then.)* All right, all right already ... You would think our home is a golf course, you know, you just would.

ARNOLD. All right, Barone.

BARONE. Oh, I know. I know ... *(A beat.)* I knew the night we first danced in your basement, and I was like 14 years old ... *(A beat.)* I knew I would be with you, Arnie. And I knew I would be alone ... *(A beat. Arnold swings the golf club. Then, Barone sighs, starts to clear away Arnold's dishes. Then stops, sits down at table. Sighs.)* Okay, I'll just sit here, and not even leave ... *(A beat.)* I mean, I'm sure he's all right. He'll be fine on his own. *(A beat.)* I mean, you know, honey, I'm sure you must know Bradley, your son ... *(A beat.)* Why should I worry his vision's so blurred from cocaine that he won't see the road? *(A beat.)* I mean, this is silence here — isn't it? This silence of yours is my home ... *(A full long beat. Then Barone readjusts herself. A moment. Then, in a whole new tone:)* Oh, honey, it'll be wonderful, won't it? Really! With Davey we'll all be together. Thanksgiving! Oh, honey, I just feel my heart running over. We just have so much to be grateful for, don't we? *(No response.)* Arnie?

ARNOLD.   What is it?

BARONE.   Oh, Arnie! We just have so much to be thankful for, don't we? *(No response.)* Arnie?

ARNOLD.   What is it?

BARONE.   Oh, Arnie, don't we? *(A beat.)*

ARNOLD.   We sure do, Barone. *(A beat. Music as Arnold swings golf club. As he reaches top of his swing BLACKOUT.)*

END OF ACT I

ENTR'ACTE I

David stands alone Onstage, spotlit.

DAVID. So okay, I came home. My Mother had said to me, "Wait there for Bradley. Be a big brother. God knows your brother could use a big brother. Wait there for Bradley and talk to him, honey." *(A beat.)* I waited around in the airport two hours. I called Brad's machine. I kept thinking I saw him. *(A beat.)* Finally I went and called my Dad up. He said he was watching a golf match on TV. He'd be there as soon as it ended. What could I say? *(A beat.)* It's funny, you know, then when he picked me up, there we were, in the smell of his new car, and again I just couldn't find anything I could say. I mean, it was real hard, watching him wanting to tell me how sick he was. *(A beat.)* Finally he said, "You know, son, I know it's like going through hell for you, coming home. Coming back here where you always were sick and stuff. Still, you don't know what it means to your Mother." *(A beat.)* Meanwhile, I could see his hand was trembling; sitting on the steering wheel trembling like a mute white thing. *(A beat.)* Again I wanted to say something to him, but once again – I don't know – I couldn't quite speak. *(A beat.)* Finally he turned to me and said, "You know, son, I always thank God that I found golf." I said, "Huh?" *(A beat.)* He said, "I'll tell you, you don't know, swinging that golf club –, it's like my own slice of eternity. Really, son." *(A beat.)*

BLACKOUT

25

BETH

ACT II

Music plays in dark; ends and lights come up on Beth standing, a mug of coffee in her hand, gazing out over the audience, as if over a lake. As if looking through the long glass windows that lead to the deck of her ten-year-old cedar wood home.

Upstage of her, and to the Left, spreads her kitchen. The central stove is built like a range, with linoleum counters around it. The unit should contain a trashmasher. Bar stools on Right side. Refrigerator behind. Sink Up Right. Up Center of this area, Right of the refrigerator, there may be doors that lead to a pantry. Upstage and to the left of Beth, there may be an ante-room, off of the kitchen, with sofa.

After some gazing over the lake, Beth has finished her coffee, looks down into empty mug. Crosses back into kitchen. Enters pantry. Emerges with box of Oreos. If no pantry, She takes them out of cabinet. Stands in kitchen, holding box, eating them. Perhaps shaking remains of box into her mouth as car horn honks. Beth starts. Swallows or spits out Oreos. Then doorbell rings. Beth opens trashmasher and tosses in box. Closes masher. Reaches for pot, as doorbell rings, and pours herself more coffee. Doorbell rings again.

NOTE: Beth uses the phrase "My life" as an exclamation like, "Wonderful," or "Great." Or she may use it as a sigh, or a curse; as if to say, "How can life be this?"

BETH.   All right. All right already. *(She lays down mug. Under her breath.)* For God's sake. *(She crosses to door U. R., and opens it. Lets in David. Beth embraces him hugely, in both arms.)* It's my life — my life, that you're here! My life!
DAVID.   Oh, Beth, you're here! I'm here!
BETH.   My life!
DAVID.   Oh, Beth, it's just amazing that we're here!
BETH.   It's great you're here.
DAVID.   Oh, Beth, it's just amazing that you're here!
BETH.   Dave, I live here.
DAVID.   Oh, yeah.
BETH.   Here, close the door. *(She goes to close it.)* Who's out there ...? Dad? Is Dad out there?
DAVID.   Yeah, Dad.
BETH.   He drove you here?
DAVID.   Uh, yeah. He did.
BETH.   So do you mean to say he wouldn't come in?
DAVID.   He said he'd be back in time to play with the girls before they lay down for their nap.
BETH.   I guess he wanted to play golf.
DAVID.   I guess.
BETH.   I guess ... *(A beat.)* Well, Dave, you might as well come in. You can forget about Dad. *(She closes the door.)* I mean, I just thought we could sit and have bagels and talk, just you and me and Dad ... I mean, I got bagels for the talk, but then, you know Dad ... I mean, well, you might as well come in. Just put down your bag. *(Calling off.)* Barry, Dave's here. *(Then, to David.)* We'll let him worry with your bag ... *(A beat. She crosses toward kitchen.)* You'll never believe the girls, Dave. They've gotten so big.
DAVID.   *(Noting Beth's obesity.)* Huh. *(A beat.)*
BETH.   Well, we could sit and have bagels without Dad, I guess.
DAVID.   No, that's okay, Beth.
BETH.   You want something to eat? I've got oatmeal —
DAVID.   Uh, well, I brought my own.
BETH.   That's fine. See, to me, that's fine. You want oatmeal, so you bring your own. But, Dave, you'll never believe this: Mom called. She said, "I've been rushing around to Sue's" —

you know, Sue Cohen, and her health foods. She said, "Well, she had the rolled oats, the steelcut oats, the Irish oats. I just didn't know which ones to get."

DAVID. I like organic whole oats.

BETH. "Organic whole oats." Uhuh, I see. Well, I didn't think of that ... *(A beat.)*

BARRY. *(Offstage calling.)* Honey, is that Dave?

BETH. *(Calling back.)* Yeah, honey, he's here. *(A beat, to David.)* Then she wanted to know what else she could get ... What you would eat she would get ... I mean, she said, "Beth, there's just so little he eats now; there's so little left ... There's just so little I can do for him; there's just so little left ... I mean, Beth, you know me: I'm his mother; there's just so little left ... I mean, I don't know what he eats; there's just so little left ... I picked up some tofu at Sue's. I got pineapple at Appleman's ... Then I don't even know if he's eating fruit; there's just so little left ... I mean, when you don't see your son, you just have to kind of guess ..." *(Barry, her husband, late 30's, somewhat overweight, sticks his head in doorway U.R.)*

BARRY. Honey, where's my Lava?

BETH. I guess where you left it.

BARRY. In the shower?

BETH. Yeah, I guess.

BARRY. *(Entering.)* Hi, Dave. I'll be back in a minute. I'm not being rude.

DAVID. I know. Hi, Barry. By the way, you're looking good.

BARRY. Yeah, that's what I say. I lose a pound, Beth gains two.

BETH. Aaah gaad — that's what I say too. *(Phone rings.)*

BARRY. Okay, guys, I'm in the Jacuzzi. Then I'm in the shower with my girls. *(Phone rings. Barry exits.)*

BETH. There she is. *(She crosses to phone.)* Do you want some coffee? Or you don't drink coffee now, do you?

DAVID. Maybe I'll just start cooking some oatmeal while you're talking.

BETH. You think she's calling for me? *(She picks up receiver, as David fetches oats from his bag. As Beth speaks she offers him pot, but he goes to his bag, and fetches his own. Then, Beth offers a spoon;*

he fetches his own, a strainer, etc. He begins rinsing and preparing oats....) Hello. Oh, hi, Mom! What a surprise. Well, guess who's here. Yeah. He got in all right. Making oatmeal. No, organic oat groats ... Mom, maybe you should ask for yourself how he is. Okay, Mom, here he is ... No, I'm fine. *(Beth lays phone on her breast. She and David exchange a look.)*

DAVID. *(Taking phone. As he speaks he continues rinsing oats, measuring water, etc.)* Hi, Mom. How are you? ... Oh. God, I'm sorry... No, it was fine. It was great ... No, I brought some ... Organic, yeah... No, oat groats. It means completely unrefined ... Mom, I don't know how oat groats grow. Maybe you could ask Sue.

BETH. It's just beyond speech.

DAVID. *(Laying phone on breast, to Beth.)* Will you listen to this?

BETH. Beyond speech.

DAVID. *(Back on phone.)* No, I was making my food ... No, fine. Fine ... Actually, no. I don't eat pineapples. I don't eat any tropical fruit ... No, they're too yin.

BETH. "Too yin."

DAVID. Too yin as opposed to too yang. The idea is that you should eat the foods that grow of the climate and location where you live. And pineapples, you know, they grow in a tropical zone. And we are all beings being in a temperate zone ... No, grains are good for everyone, no matter what zone ... Mom, my oatmeal's cooking. I need it for this zone ... Okay ... So we'll see you later. Right. Okay. *(Still holding phone.)* Beth, do you have something else to say to Mom? *(Beth looks at David; one look as if to say "Are you kidding?")* No. *(Beth sighs.)* Okay. Okay, Mom. My oatmeal — Bye bye. *(He hangs up the receiver.)* It never changes.

BETH. *(After a look of agreement.)* What did she ask about the girls?

DAVID. Just whether they were sleeping.

BETH. You'd never believe it. How I live.

BETTY. *(Offstage.)* Mommy ... Mommy ...

BETH. What is it, honey?

BETTY. *(Offstage.)* Mommy —

BETH. *(Calling back.)* Yes, honey, what is it?

BETTY. *(Running on.)* Mommy —
BETH. That's Betty.
BETTY. *(Running in, wrapped in a towel.)* Mommy, Mommy, is he here? Is he here?
BETH. He is. Here he is.
BETTY. *(Embarrassed.)* Hello, Uncle Dave.
DAVID. Did you just get out of the shower?
BETTY. Yeah. With my Dad.
DAVID. Will you give me a kiss? *(As Betty kisses David.)*
BETH. Can you believe it? Here it is, my life.
DAVID. *(To Betty.)* How are you doing?
BETTY. Fine.
DAVID. And how is school going?
BETTY. Fine. Mommy said that you can talk in French.
DAVID. Is that what Mommy said?
BETTY. I'm learning French, Uncle Dave.
DAVID. Really? Does the teacher teach in French?
BETTY. Huh?
DAVID. Or does she just speak in English?
BETTY. In English I guess. Yeah.
DAVID. Je crois que c'est tres important que tu entends la langue comme elle est parlee ... Comme ca, tu vois?
BETTY. *(After a beat, for thought.)* Yeah. Do you live in New York?
BETH. You know he does, honey.
BETTY. Have you been to the Statue of Liberty?
DAVID. I have.
BETTY. Have you been to the top?
DAVID. Maybe I'll save that for when you come to visit.
BETTY. When's that?
DAVID. Talk to your mommy.
BARRY. *(Offstage.)* Honey, where did Dani put my blue shirt?
BETH. Which blue shirt?
BARRY. *(Offstage.)* My Lacoste. *(A beat.)*
BETH. I don't know, honey. *(Barry enters, perhaps with drink in hand, still wrapped in bath towel.)*
BARRY. That Dani, I'll tell you, she has her way here. I mean, Dave, I'll tell ya, you never figure when you marry a nice

31

Jewish girl, you're also marrying the maid who was trained by her mom.

DAVID. *(To Beth.)* So you have Dani Ann here?

BETH. Once a week for God's sake.

BARRY. What you cooking, Dave?

DAVID. It's oatmeal.

BARRY. Oatmeal?

DAVID. Organic oat groats.

BARRY. *(Looking in the refrigerator.)* What have we got in the box to eat, honey?

BETH. I don't know, honey ... Betty, go downstairs and take a look in on Becky, before you put your clothes on. Will you do that for Mommy?

BETTY. Will you help me, Mommy?

BETH. I will, honey. *(Betty exits.)*

BARRY. Honey, what's for dinner?

BETH. I don't know, honey.

BARRY. We've got Stubbs type white chocolate. Would you like some white chocolate, Dave?

DAVID. No, thank you.

BARRY. *(Standing in the refrigerator door, eating white chocolate.)* You know, I love this stuff. You hate yourself for eating it, but you know, I just love it. The way I figure it's like this, okay? It's like, there's just got to be a limit to how much weight you can gain in a day. It's like, how many units of heat can your body take? The way I figure it, there's got to be a limit to the number of calories your body can assimilate. So that way you can have your pig days and your starve days. You know, you hear about these guys, these Liz Taylor types, who tell you they dieted all week, and then they just binged out all day. And that one day didn't seem to make a difference. This is how I figure it. They say there's thirty-two hundred calories that make up a pound. Say if you eat thirty-two hundred calories and get no exercise, you'll gain one pound that day. Or if you eat sixty-four hundred calories, two pounds that day. But let's say you eat just all the sugary stuff — all the Pepperidge Farm Milano cookies, all the Sarah Lee cakes, all the boxes you can find of Sugar Frosted Flakes — let's say you just eat up all that stuff in one day — I mean, there's still just got to be a limit to how much of that weight your body can put on in that day ...

DAVID.   Huh ...

BARRY.   I'll tell ya, Dave, last night I could barely sleep, just imagining all the stuff I could eat today. It's like this Stubbs type white chocolate. I mean, I'll tell ya, you can just about taste this stuff in your teeth. It's got this great like vanilla type taste ... You sure you don't want some, Dave?

DAVID.   No, today is my starve day.

BARRY.   Not mine, Dave. You know, I'm in between sizes now in my Levis. I figure it's just as easy now to go for the forty as for the thirty-eight. Honey, isn't that right? *(No response.)* Honey, isn't that right? *(A silence.)* Honey, where are my Nilla Wafers?

BETH.   What, honey?

BARRY.   My Nilla Wafers.

BETH.   I don't know, honey.

BARRY.   The Oreos are gone, I know that. *(Pause.)*

BETH.   Honey, let me go help Betty put on her clothes, okay? *(She exits.)*

BARRY.   *(To Beth, as she goes.)* Okay. *(To David.)* So how's New York treating you, Dave? *(Barry's seated, with his bath towel wrapped around him, David cooking oatmeal; Barry pours himself a drink, or refreshes his drink.)*

DAVID.   It's great.

BARRY.   It is? *(Lowering his voice.)* Dave, talk to your sister.

DAVID.   What?

BARRY.   You're the only one left.

DAVID.   Huh?

BARRY.   Talk to her. I have. Your mom has.

DAVID.   What about?

BARRY.   Her weight.

DAVID.   Why should I? What would I say?

BARRY.   I don't know, Dave. *(A beat.)* I don't know what it is. She just keeps getting bigger and bigger. I go out — I know there's a box of Oreos in the cupboard, I come back and it's gone. It's like she hides it.

DAVID. Oh.

BARRY. Or I open the trash-masher, there's a sack of Vienna fingers, an empty bag, and I know I haven't seen any Vienna fingers ... Last weekend, you know, I found a pack of Tootsie Pop Drops, stashed in with the baby's diapers ...

DAVID. You know, I've never said anything to her. I thought I'd always be the one person who just wouldn't bother her. I mean, Barry, when I was so sick as a kid, Beth was like my only friend. I mean, I don't know if I can violate the quiet we still have.

BARRY. You're our last hope, Dave.

DAVID. I don't know, Bar.

BARRY. But, Dave, she sees how well you've done, with your macrobiotics. Don't you want to share that stuff with us? *(A beat.)* Who's worth it, if not your sister, Dave? It's not just how she looks. It's her health and happiness.

DAVID. I know that.

BARRY. I mean, can you imagine the kind of strain that weight is putting on her heart? And now this year, what with her accident, what kind of strain is all that stomach putting on her back?

DAVID. I don't know.

BARRY. Just talk to her, Dave. You're her brother. She'll listen.

DAVID. Well, maybe I could say something to her about macrobiotics ...

BARRY. You will?

DAVID. I'll try.

BARRY. Do more than try.

DAVID. Okay. I'll try.

BARRY. That's just great, Dave. Great. Can I fix you a drink?

DAVID. No, that's okay ... *(Beth re-enters.)*

BARRY. You know, if there's anything else I can ever tell you about the business, Dave, just let me know. *(Beth re-enters with basket of yellow feathers and chicken costume.)*

DAVID. So how is it going there with Brad?

BETH. *(Under her breath.)* Ha —

BARRY. *(A beat.)* Honey, tell your brother Dave about when

we had them over for Hanukkah ...

BETH. I will, honey. The first night of Hanukkah ...

BARRY. *(Interrupting.)* Dave, do you know? Do you ever see your brother doing cocaine?

DAVID. No — I don't see him. I don't know if they do it. Maybe they just wouldn't do it in front of me.

BARRY. Uh huh.

DAVID. I don't know. *(A beat.)* You know, the thing is, I keep trying to talk to them both about macrobiotics.

BARRY. Dave, I would like to read that book you've got on macrobiotics.

DAVID. You'd be welcome to it.

BARRY. I mean, we are starting to eat a lot less red meat now, aren't we, honey?

BETH. Yeah. We're getting into it.

BARRY. I'm starting to carb-up.

DAVID. What?

BARRY. Carb-up. You know, that's what we call it, in these parts, loading up on carbohydrates.

DAVID. "Carbing-up."

BETH. The gross thing is, I'll be shopping at Appleman's —

BARRY. Speaking of carbohydrates —

DAVID. What?

BARRY. Honey, didn't we buy Hydrox?

BETH. What?

BARRY. Hydrox? They don't have all those preservatives, like Oreos. The rabbis bless them or something.

BETH. Aaah gaad —

BARRY. I could've sworn we bought Oreos or Hydrox. Honey, what could we have done with them?

BETH. Aaah gaad. I haven't seen them, for God's sake.

BARRY. She hasn't seen them, for God's sake. You heard that?

BETH. Just stop it. For God's sake, just stop it.

BARRY. All right, babe.

BETH. Sometimes he gets gross like this after a shower.

BARRY. Dave, talk to your sister.

DAVID. What?

BARRY. You know, like you told me, there was something so

big you wanted so much to sit and talk to her about.

DAVID. What?

BARRY. You know, Dave ... *(He exits.)*

BETH. Aaah gaad — Aaah gaad —

DAVID. Aaah gaad — Aaah gaad —

BETH. Aaah gaad — Aaah gaad — Let's just move over here. I have to sew these feathers onto Barbara's costume for the school dance recital. She's going as Chicken Little. Yesterday I was chasing all around the house for these yellow feathers. I thought, is this my life? I thought, "The sky is falling. The sky is falling." *(A beat.)* So what did you want to tell me? *(Horn honks.)*

DAVID. What's that?

BETH. It's Mamoo.

DAVID. What?

BETH. Mamoo. Just wait and see if it isn't Mamoo.

DAVID. "Mamoo ..." *(Doorbell rings, one long insistent ring.)*

BETH. *(A sigh.)* My life. *(Getting up.)* My life with Mamoo ... *(She goes to door, opens it.)*

BARONE. *(In door.)* Hi, doll. Oh, where is he?

BETH. Who?

BARONE. "Who?"!

DAVID. *(Standing.)* Hi, Mom.

BARONE. My baby, let me look at you.

BETH. Aaah gaad. *(As David goes to his Mom, and she embraces him.)*

BARONE. I just know there's a God sometimes when I hold you.

DAVID. What else are you holding?

BARONE. The pineapple. Oh, God, the pineapple! Well, I didn't know what to do with it. I mean, I know you don't eat fruit like this. It's too yin — I know it. I know it. But I just didn't know what you could find to eat in this house if you got hungry. *(A beat.)* Beth, I brought that rattatouille. I told Barry to bring it in. I brought the rest of that brisket. I thought you might want it. I don't know if Brad and Candi are dropping by — whoever knows when they'll show up? But I thought, I mean, I just thought I had to invite them.

BETH. Aaah gaad.

BARONE. *(To David.)* My baby, let me look at you ... *(Then.)* The grey in your hair looks so distinguished!

DAVID. Okay, Mom.

BARONE. *(Embracing him again.)* My heart. I'm holding my heart. It's here ...

DAVID. Okay, Mom.

BARONE. *(Still holding on to him, but standing more apart.)* I brought you some tofu.

DAVID. That's great.

BARONE. *(To him alone.)* She just never has a thing in her house to eat. I don't know how you can be raising kids, without at least an apple in the box. Oh, you're just my heart. I am holding my heart here ... *(As she embraces him a last time.)* Equal to the birth, your coming. Equal to the birth of another child for Beth is your coming back here ... Oh, you just feel so warm ... *(Then to Beth.)* Doll, we just have this moment. One moment while Barry's still out there with the brisket. Before your father comes in here — wanting his tea or whatever ...

BETH. Okay, what is it?

BARONE. Doll ... *(To David.)* Do you see it, David? How she wrinkles her face like that? She could be beautiful ... *(To Beth.)* You'll never know, the day you were born — how it made me happy, to have a daughter ...

BETH. Maybe I know, Mom. I have a daughter.

BARONE. *(To Beth.)* Doll, I want you to listen to me. I want you to come with me.

BETH. Where, Mom?

BARONE. To the spa, doll. For two weeks. Leave Barry and the kids. It's just two weeks of nothing but you.

BETH. Who is that, Mom?

BARONE. Nobody else to think about but you ... First your message, then your work-out. Then they're rushing you off for your facial. The strawberry, the raspberry facial! Then the mud masks! Each day you keep wondering how can you fit it all in — the massage, and the facial ... And then, all the meals! I mean, it's all simply gourmet food. Low calories, it's true; but you'd never believe it. The fruit mousse! You would love that fruit mousse, David. Or is it too yin, mousse?

DAVID.   Depends on the fruit.

BETH.   Let's open that pineapple.

BARONE.   What do you say, doll? *(Doorbell rings.)*

BETH.   Aaah gaad —

BARONE.   It must be your father. *(Beth goes to door. Aside, to David.)* Do me a favor, David.

DAVID.   What's that?

BARONE.   Just give me a moment later when I can talk to you ...

BETH.   *(Opening door.)* Hi, Dad.

ARNOLD.   Hi, doll. *(Beth and Arnold embrace, then.)* Doll, you look great. You've lost some weight.

BETH.   Aaah gaad —

BARONE.   Arnie, have you got that cornbread?

ARNOLD.   I have, dear.

DAVID.   What cornbread?

BARONE.   I made us all some macrobiotic cornbread.

BETH.   Aaah gaad —

ARNOLD.   Who's that skinny boy over there?

DAVID.   Hi, Dad.

ARNOLD.   Gosh, you look great. *(David and Arnold embrace, then stand apart, at arm's length.)*

BARONE.   Here, dear, give me the cornbread.

ARNOLD.   Dave, you look great. I think you must have put on a little weight.

BETH.   Can I get you something to drink, Dad?

BARONE.   Just give me the cornbread, honey.

ARNOLD.   All right.

BARONE.   I'll set it down here by your oatmeal, honey.

ARNOLD.   You know, doll, maybe your old man could use a little tea.

BETH.   "My life!"

ARNOLD.   You know, I think this house is great.

BARONE.   So this is what organic oat groats look like.

ARNOLD.   I know when you kids were building it, I must have said, how can you build a quarter-of-a-million-dollar house like that, your age — and out on a lake. And your mom, you know —

BARONE. Who?

ARNOLD. Well, your Mom is your Mom. And she was just worried, what with the dust and the grass, you'd get asthma attacks.

BARONE. I'll always be your mother.

BARRY. *(Entering.)* Beth, I've got that brisket.

BETH. Come on in.

ARNOLD. But now I'm convinced this house is great. Looking out like you can over that lake. *(Phone rings.)*

BETH. Now who the hell is that? *(She crosses back to answer phone.)*

BARONE. *(To David.)* David, I want you to listen to me.

DAVID. What is it?

BETH. *(Answering phone.)* Hello. Oh, hi, Candi. How are you feeling? Yeah ... Mom and Dad just got here. *(Mouths to her mother.)* It's Candi.

BARONE. This saga!

BETH. *(Back to Candi.)* So what did he say about the splint? In Dallas? In Dallas. Yeah, and so what did he say? Yeah. Oh, I know ... I know ... *(As Beth's talking to Candi, Barone's talking to David; their speeches overlap.)*

BARONE. It's not even worth talking about, this saga. *(Pulling David aside.)* David, I want you to talk to her.

DAVID. What?

BARONE. You're the only one left. David, do this for your mother. You know, I swore I'd never speak to her again about her weight. I don't know what it is — why I should alienate her. But she just won't listen to me anymore. I think maybe it's because I've kept my figure. I think she resents it, my staying so thin. Just like I was her competitor.

BETH. *(Continuing on phone with Candi.)* Okay then, I'll expect you. No, thanks. You know, Mom brought a brisket and whatever. Oh, I know ... No, really, thank you. Okay, I'll see you ...

BARONE. Promise me, David. Promise me.

DAVID. All right already.

BARONE. Make this promise to your mother.

DAVID. All right then.

39

BARONE. *(As Beth's hanging up phone.)* Honey, your water's boiling.

BETH. Just a minute. *(Into phone.)* Okay, Candi, see you. *(She hangs up.)*

ARNOLD. Who was that?

BARONE. It's Brad and Candi, honey. *(To Beth.)* Honey, your water's boiling.

BETH. All right.

BARONE. So, where are they?

BETH. They're just around the corner. *(To herself.)* My life!

DAVID. I'll get that teabag for you.

BARRY. Baroney, you mind if I taste this brisket?

BARONE. Just save some for dinner, honey.

BARRY. All right.

DAVID. He's having a pig day.

BETH. Aaah gaad —

BARONE. So where are they, at that pharmacy?

BETH. Yeah.

BARRY. Filling another prescription for Perkodan, I'll bet.

BARONE. I just can't talk about this.

BARRY. You know, that girl's just become an addict. Our friend Catrell works down at Helfricht Clinic — at the clinic for eating disorders — and she said, in nine out of ten cases of anorexia, there's a chemical dependency ...

BETH. You want cream and sugar in this, Dad?

ARNOLD. Unless you've got some of that artificial sweetener.

BARONE. Barry, I don't know. Maybe you can talk to her. She just looks like she's about to just drop. You know those days you feel like you're about to just drop? Well, that's how she looks. You know, like about to just drop.

BETH. Well, she never eats anything. The other night they were here. What did she eat? Two of those Pepperidge Farm rye rounds and a bit of cheese.

BARRY. She likes those Amstel Lights.

BARONE. I can feel she'll just drop. We'll see, she'll just drop.

BETH. Have we got any in there, honey?

BARONE. She'll just drop. A person can't live on beer and brownies.

DAVID. You mean, all she eats is beer and brownies?

BETH. Haven't you heard that shit about how her mom just gave her a Reese's cup and a Coke for breakfast, when she was growing up?

BARONE. Honey, I'm dropping, just listening.

DAVID. It's funny. I call her. I talked to her for hours when she was down there in Florida, having her surgery on her jaw. And every day I'd talk about miso soup, and brown rice, and she'd say, "Yeah. Oh, yeah. Now, you know, that makes sense to me ..."

BETH. They're just so full of shit.

BARONE. I'm plotzing.

DAVID. It makes it hard to talk to them.

BARONE. You just don't know what it does to me, to stand and hear this.

DAVID. You're plotzing.

BETH. The one I feel so badly for is Brian. I mean, Dave, weeks and weeks can go by, and they just don't bother to drive him to kindergarten.

BARONE. You just don't know what this does to me.

ARNOLD. Your mother is plotzing.

BETH. You just can't do that with a child like that. That school's the best thing in his life. The other day, I mean, I came to pick up Barbara —

BARONE. *(Interrupting Beth.)* Dave doesn't know, honey, Brian's in the same class with Barbara. I've got pictures at home of them dressed up like chickens, at Easter, I'll show you ...

BETH. *(Offended that she's been interrupted.)* And anyway, the teacher said to me, Dave, it had been so long since she'd seen Brian, she'd basically forgotten what he looked like.

ARNOLD. How's that tea coming?

DAVID. I'll get it.

BARRY. *(Pouring himself a drink.)* Have we told you the story of last Hanukkah, Dave?

BETH. The first night of Hanukkah —

BARONE. Barry, can't we save this for later?

DAVID. *(With teacup, by his dad.)* Here's your tea, Dad.

ARNOLD. Thank you, son.

41

BETH.   Honey, look and see if we've got any of that Amstel Light for Candi. *(Barry exits. Arnold takes David, in his arms, before him, and stands behind him, each looking out over lake together, gently swaying, David still holding mug of tea.)*

BARONE.   Honey, I'm sorry I invited them over; I'm plotzing ... I didn't know it would have to turn into such a circus. I'm sorry ...

BETH.   It's all right.

BARONE.   I just thought — with Dave coming home, we could all be together.

BETH.   Act like a regular family?

BARONE.   Honey, all you've got's your family ... I just thought that we could all be together again; and sit around and visit with each other, like a family ... *(A beat, as Beth pulls or turns away.)* I don't know, I thought you'd want to see your brother. I never had a brother or a sister to talk to. I always thought, if I just had someone to talk to ... After Mother died, I just had no one to talk to ...

BARRY.   *(Re-entering with Amstel Lights.)* Have we told you the story of last Hanukkah, Dave?

BETH.   The first night of Hanukkah ...

BARONE.   Barry, can't we save this for later? *(Barry crosses back into kitchen area.)*

DAVID.   What are you thinking about, looking out on the lake like this?

ARNOLD.   Oh, I don't know ... You know, sometimes I wish you kids were still the size of that girl in the Coppertone ad — you know, with the dog pulling her towel from behind ...

DAVID.   You do? Why?

BARONE.   He just was never there when you kids were kids.

ARNOLD.   You just never know, son, it's all going to go so fast.

BARONE.   When we got married we were just still such kids.

ARNOLD.   And I just kept myself so damn busy, getting down to open the doors of that store by eight, and staying there till I'd come home to have our dinner —

BARONE.   Our one time together.

ARNOLD.   And then I'd be back at the books, and making

out the checks ... And you know, somehow you never figure, you're never going to get that chance again — to play with your kids when they're still there like your kids.

BARONE.   I watched it happen ...

ARNOLD.   And then one day it's like, poof — they're just not there. And that dollar you worked so hard to lay aside for their education — is paying their college tuition, and you're just the guy they call up and ask to send checks. *(A beat.)* And then, you know, sometimes I guess you just have to wonder, if I hadn't done all that, if I hadn't kept myself so damn busy, down at the store all those years, would I have been able to give you kids all I can? I mean, who would've dreamed that I would stand in my daughter's quarter-of-a-million-dollar house, and just stand here, with my tea getting cold, looking out on her lake like this ...?

BETTY.   *(Running on.)* Papi — Papi —

ARNOLD.   Now, who's that calling out to Papi?

BETTY.   Papi —   *(Arnold lets go of David to embrace Betty.)*

DAVID.   I'll hold your tea cup for you, Dad.

ARNOLD.   Now, who's there?

BETTY.   Papi!

ARNOLD.   My baby — Betty — do you know the story of how the lake ever got there?

BETTY.   Tell me, Papi.

BETH.   *(To David, overlapping as Arnold speaks to Betty.)* Can you believe my life came out like this? My life ... Just put down the tea here.

BARONE.   *(As Arnold and Betty continue.)* He's just like a changed man.

BARRY.   You know, Baroney, this brisket is not too bad. Maybe we could use you on Mondays and Fridays to cook it.

BARONE.   I'd cost more than Dani ...

BETH.   Aaah gaad —

BARONE.   I've just had more experience. I guess in those days we girls used to cook for our families, for our husbands.

BETH.   Aaah gaad. Now I just give them a slice of Velveeta. Dave, are you sure you don't want one? Aaah gaad —

BARONE.   God, do you kids remember the years of cooking

43

the weekly briskets ... ? The pot roasts — the lamb chops —
DAVID. You made me eat it.
BARONE. *(Having moved over to Dave, arm around him.)* Honey
... *(A beat.)* At least we had dinners. *(Aside to David.)* I mean,
David, talk to your sister. She just gives those kids like a fish
stick — a slice of cheese. I mean, you heard her say, "Velveeta."
I mean, you just can't raise kids like that —
BETH. Dave, I think your oatmeal's burning.
DAVID. Have you got any Velveeta?
BARRY. Baroney — I want you guys to see something. Arnie.
Now, listen to this. I come in this morning; I say, "Honey, where
are my Oreos?" Now, Dave is my witness. Dave, what did she
say?
DAVID. I can't remember.
BARRY. She said, "I just haven't seen them, honey."
BETH. Did anybody tape it?
BARRY. Now, look at this, Baroney. *(He produces a box of Oreos
from trash-masher.)* Look what I found in the trash-masher, Bar-
oney.
BETH. For God's sake.
BARRY. A rumpled box of Oreos — empty. *(Doorbell rings.)*
BARONE. It's Brad and Candi.
BETH. For God's sake.
BARRY. Dave, you'll be my witness. You were here. I come in
here this morning, I say to her, "Honey, where are my Oreos?"
There's silence. I say, "Honey?" She says, "I haven't seen them,
honey."
BARONE. Enough, Barry.
BRADLEY. *(Swinging open door and striding in, Candi behind him.)*
Hey, babe.
BETH. *(Chanting as she hugs him.)* Hey —
BRADLEY. This babe has got a sweet ass, doesn't she, Candi?
BETH. *(Greeting her.)* How you doin', Candi?
CANDI. Just fine.
BETH. *(Seeing large, tin-foil wrapped baking dish in Candi's arms.)*
Did you bring me something?
BRADLEY. Candi made some of her yams.
BARONE. *(From where she was.)* God love her.

BARRY.　What would we do without 'em?

BRADLEY.　Look out, it's my brother.

DAVID.　*(As Bradley embraces him.)* Hi, Brad.

BETH.　*(With yams she's taken from Candi.)* Just let me set these down here.

BARRY.　*(Still at brisket.)* What's that, hon?

BETH.　Candi made some yams for us.

CANDI.　It was just nothing.

BETH.　Can I fix you guys something to drink?

CANDI.　Look at these two hugging.

BETTY.　Papi, it's Uncle Bradley.

ARNOLD.　It is. Let's go see Uncle Bradley.

BARONE.　You don't know what it means to me, here; here, you guys — behind my eyes here — here, as your mother — to see my boys standing together again, like grown-ups now, and hugging ... I guess I must have done something right as a mother ... *(Then, to Beth.)* Here, honey, put the yams here.

BRADLEY.　God, you look so good, David.

DAVID.　I've gotten healthy.

BRADLEY.　You just look so good, man.

DAVID.　Yeah, so do you.

ARNOLD.　Brad, I think you've taken off those few pounds you put on after you quit smoking.

BARONE.　It was just in his belly, honey.

BETH.　Aaah gaad — Aaah gaad —

BARRY.　I bet somebody here could use an Amstel Light.

CANDI.　You bet I could.

BETTY.　Mommy — Mommy —

BETH.　What is it, honey?

BETTY.　Mommy, Mommy, I think I killed Becky.

BETH.　I'll go look with you, honey. Just give me a minute.

BARONE.　I'll turn on the oven.

BETH.　Why's that, Mom?

BARONE.　To keep Candi's yams warm, honey.

BARRY.　Can I try one of those, Candi?

CANDI.　Sure you can, Barry.

BARONE.　Let's wait till we all get hungry.

BRADLEY.　*(To David.)* Okay, man, tell me about it.

ARNOLD. Just let me get my hug, son. *(To David, as he embraces Bradley.)* You know, this is my other son.

DAVID. Yeah? Tell me about it.

BETH. Come on with me, Betty. *(She exits with Betty.)*

BARONE. I just want my own hug.

BARRY. *(Pouring her a beer.)* Now, Candi, when do we hug?

CANDI. Barry, that's enough now.

BARONE. This just is what it all is. This is what life has. I'm sorry I put everybody out. I'm sorry I made everybody worry —

BARRY. No need to be sorry, Baroney.

BARONE. But I just thought we all had to be together like a family. I guess this is the happiness you come to. This is all the happiness God gives you as a mother. I never had a sister or a brother. Now this is my moment to gather the rosebuds, to look at my boys here — here, with their sister: my own little bluebird of happiness, my one daughter ... This is the moment I feel like I have done something ...

ARNOLD. *(Touching her.)* And what about your husband?

BARONE. Honey, will you get me my camera? I want to remember this. I want to get some pictures.

BARRY. So who else is hungry?

BARONE. Maybe Beth's got some cheese or something she can lay out here, so we don't have to sit down this instant to dinner. I just want to get you guys in a few of my pictures.

BETH. *(Entering.)* What's going on here?

BARRY. Your mom's taking pictures.

BRADLEY. *(To David.)* Sit down and talk to me.

DAVID. Just let me stir my oatmeal. *(Bradley crosses to David.)*

ARNOLD. Where'd Betty go, honey?

BETH. She went down to look after Becky.

BARONE. *(Back, with camera, aiming it at David as he stirs oatmeal.)* Okay, honey, just smile, here.

DAVID. No, Mom.

BARONE. Honey, just smile for your mother.

DAVID. Can't you take mine later?

BARONE. Honey —

DAVID. Why do we have to keep staging our lives for you pictures?

BARONE. *(A long uncomfortable beat, then.)* David, I'm your mother. You don't know what it will be like for me when you've gone back to New York. What will I have when I sit there on the sofa and try to remember? Meanwhile he'll just be there swinging the golf club. Just one for your mother ...? *(A beat.)*

DAVID. All right.

BARONE. Here, Beth, get into the picture.

BETH. *(Joining her brothers.)* Aaah gaad —

BARONE. *(She tries to snap the picture.)* Damn it. This damn camera. Honey — Just hold still, Dave.

DAVID. Mom —

BARONE. Just a minute. This damn camera again. I just can't get the flash to work on it ... *(Beth and Bradley move away the minute they see the camera won't work.)*

ARNOLD. Let me look at it, honey. *(He takes camera, examines it.)*

BARRY. *(Standing with Candi at brisket.)* You know, Candi, I used to think that you just didn't like to eat. But now I hear that you would eat, you'd like to, except that your teeth make it difficult —

CANDI. It makes it hard to chew like.

BARONE. *(Back with camera poised.)* Okay — just a minute — *(They pose, Barone flashes camera. Then.)* Okay, hold on a minute. I know how to rewind it.

DAVID. That's enough!

BARONE. I'm afraid I cut your head off, honey. God, do you kids remember the year at Hanukkah I cut everybody's head off? What could I send to your Bobi but these pictures of my children with their heads off? Okay — Okay, now. Smile, honey. *(She snaps another picture.)*

DAVID. Okay, that's it.

BARRY. Listen to this, types.

BARONE. All right, Barry, we're listening.

BETH. Have you got enough tea, Dad?

ARNOLD. I do, doll.

BARRY. All right, types.

BARONE. We'll just wait a little bit for more pictures ...

BARRY. Listen, guys.

47

DAVID.   We're listening.

BARRY.   Right. The other night, we wake up in the middle of the night

BETH.   Aaah gaad —

BARRY.   Your little niece, Dave, Barbie, has been crying —

BETH.   Aaah gaad —

BARRY.   So your sister says to me, "Okay, I'll get it —   "

BETH.   Can you imagine him getting out of bed at night?

BARRY.   So I say, "Fine, doll."

BETH.   "Fine, doll."

BARRY.   So I roll over — act like I'm sleeping. And your sister comes back in, Dave. I hear this kind of rustling plastic paper — you know the type?

BETH.   For God's sake, he knows the type.

BARRY.   So I say, "Honey, what's that rustling?"

BETH.   "That rustling."

BARRY.   And she says, "It's nothing, honey. I'm getting a cough drop."

BRADLEY.   *(To Candi.)* A cough drop! Can you believe that?

BARRY.   And so I just flash on my flashlight.

DAVID.   Your flashlight?

BETH.   The queerest part is that he hid a flashlight.

BARRY.   Well, what would you do, Arn, every night your wife just made this rustling type?

ARNOLD.   I don't know, Bar.

BARRY.   Wouldn't you lay up a flashlight?

CANDI.   *(To Bradley.)* A flashlight! Can you believe that?

BARONE.   So what did you see, Barry?

BETH.   Aaah gaad —

BARRY.   There was your sister, with her hand in the drawer of the cabinet. And what did she have in it? A half-eaten bag of those foil-wrapped Hershey's Kisses — I mean, you know the type? I mean, your sister, Dave, had hidden a bag of Kisses —

CANDI.   *(To Brad.)* Can you believe that?

BETH.   The queerest part is that he hid a flashlight. *(A beat.)*

DAVID.   Remember Hershey's Kisses? God, I remember when we were kids we used to eat them; and sometimes the foil would get caught in the chocolate and so you'd get that in your

48

teeth, and then when you would bite down on your fillings, you'd just feel this pain like slice up in your brain; you'd just want to cry out from your rib cage ... *(A beat.)*

BARONE. I can't believe this happened.

BRADLEY. *(To Candi.)* She must not be getting any.

CANDI. *(To Bradley.)* Well, can you believe that, that he could tell a story like that in front of her — your sister? I mean, I want to excuse myself, for her sake.

BRADLEY. I'll go with you, Tits.

CANDI. *(To Bradley.)* I mean, how can you sit and listen to a guy like this? *(To all — as she rises.)* Excuse me, guys.

BARONE. Just going out for a — smoke?

CANDI. I just want one cigarette.

BETH. *(As Candi exits, onto porch, with Bradley.)* Fine. *(A beat.)*

BARRY. Well, I'll tell you guys, we have got one type here who'd rather go out for a smoke than eat Baroney's brisket.

BETH. "It makes it hard to chew like." Did you hear that?

BARONE. *(To David.)* Honey, give your oat groats some water. I want to talk to you.

DAVID. Okay, just a minute, Mom.

BARRY. *(Not even turning toward them.)* Dave, talk to your mother.

DAVID. All right. *(Barone takes David aside; her conversation with him overlaps with Arnold's and Beth's.)*

BARRY. I'll tell you, Arn, I talked to Brad. I opened the phone book. I showed him the number for the clinic of eating disorders at Helfricht Hospital.

ARNOLD. It's just a bad situation.

BETH. But I mean, she could drink milk shakes — something. She could eat scrambled eggs. A person can't live like that. She gets no protein.

BARRY. Let me go talk to those guys over there.

DAVID. *(Standing apart with his mother.)* What is it?

BARONE. Honey, I'm going to take your Dad and Barry out on the deck, and I want you to talk to your sister. This is your chance, now, to talk to her.

DAVID. All right, Mom.

BARONE. All right?

49

DAVID. Well, we'll see — it's just that —

BARONE. What?

DAVID. I don't want to hurt her.

BETH. What are you plotting, guys?

BARRY. Let me go talk to those guys. *(He goes over.)*

BETH. Aaah gaad. You want some tea, Dad?

ARNOLD. I'm fine.

BETH. Some crackers?

ARNOLD. Don't want to spoil my appetite.

BETH. Aaah gaad —

BARRY. *(Now standing with David and Barone.)* Now, Dave, are you listening to what your mom's saying? I mean, you're the one who can get to her, Dave. *(Bradley and Candi re-enter.)*

BRADLEY. Well, I guess we better be going.

BARONE. What?

CANDI. We just thought Beth must be getting tired.

BRADLEY. We just dropped the kids off for an hour.

BARONE. You "better be going"? What do you mean, you better be going? We haven't even sat down to dinner.

CANDI. To dinner?

BRADLEY. Is that what life is?

BARONE. It isn't a question of what life is. Didn't I ask you kids to come over here for dinner?

BRADLEY. Hey, babe, I don't know. I mean, we just dropped the kids off with Pammy.

BARRY. Oh, did you?

ARNOLD. Honey, if they just dropped their kids off —

BARONE. Now, I'm so unhappy.

BETH. Aaah gaad, this existence.

CANDI. I mean, lately, with my teeth and stuff, sometimes we just find, I mean, you know you love to have 'em, just to be with your kids, but sometimes, well, you just can't keep running all day and night. I mean, a person gets tired. And then that's just when Brian wants you to sit down and color ...

BETH. Aaah gaad, don't I understand.

BRADLEY. We're glad to have Pammy.

BARONE. Brad, just do one favor for your mother.

BRADLEY. What's that, babe?

BARONE. Just sit down with your brother one minute — just sit down for one dinner. You'll never know till you're my age how much it means to have your children with you ...
BRADLEY. I'd like to, Sweet Ass. But, what do you think, Tits?
BARONE. Give your poor mother this one moment of fullness. Listen to me, Bradley, you don't know — you don't know what it is — what you'd do for your children. Come to that, you'd just lay down and die for them, you just would ...
BRADLEY. I know, Mom.
BETH. Can't you just call Pammy, and say you'll stay another hour?
CANDI. All right, Brad.
BRADLEY. Okay, Mom, we'll stay an hour.
BARONE. What have I done to God that he gave me such children? They make me so happy.
BETH. You hear it?
BARONE. Sometimes I want to bend down on my knees, on my knees on the stones of Jerusalem, and just thank God he could give me such children.
BETH. Can you all hear it?
BARONE. Of course, I could never get your father to go to Jerusalem.
BARRY. Let's warm up the brisket.
BARONE. That you, Brad, should say you will sit down and join us for dinner. I just can't believe I am living right here through this instant.
BETH. You want some more tea, Dad?
BARONE. I just want to get my camera. Just give me an instant.
BRADLEY. So what do you think, Tits?
ARNOLD. Doll, I'm afraid if I drink any more of this tea, I won't have any room left.
CANDI. I just don't know, Brad.
DAVID. Have you guys got any beans here, or something like that?
BARONE. Honey, look up from your oat groats and smile just like that. *(She snaps the picture.)*
CANDI. Beth, I'll just bet we're pooping you out now.

BETH.   I'm fine.

CANDI.   I'll just bet.

BARONE.   Beth, just stand by your brother like that.

CANDI.   I know a person has to sit down and rest —

BRADLEY.   Well, you know, with her back ...

CANDI.   I mean, it's just fine by me if we don't even eat. We can just sit down and sit.

BRADLEY.   You know, the thing is to visit.

ARNOLD.   It's great with you kids.

CANDI.   I mean, first you've got to set out the plates —

BETH.   I am fine, Candi.

CANDI.   Then you just set out the yams —

BETH.   I'm not tired, really.

BARONE.   *(Still posing others before camera.)* Beth —

CANDI.   And then when everyone's finished they've left such a mess.

BARRY.   *(Calling from cupboard.)* Dave, we have got some lentil soup, how about that?

BETH.   It's okay, Candi.

BARONE.   *(Posing her.)* Beth —

BRADLEY.   *(To his mother.)* How about hankering in one of me with my dad? *(Barone snaps picture.)*

DAVID.   What do you mean, it's already soup? Is it in a can?

BARONE.   It's that Chunkie soup.

BRADLEY.   I'll bet. *(To David.)* You know she just warms her children's food out of a can.

BARRY.   It says "natural," Dave.

CANDI.   I'll just set out the yams.

ARNOLD.   Now why don't you tell me again, Candi, how you make those yams?

BARONE.   Doll, I'll just turn on the oven.

BETH.   *(Over the limit; she has had enough.)* You know, that is it.

CANDI.   Well, first you skin the yams —

BARRY.   Okay, Baroney, step back. *(His line stops all but Candi. Everyone steps back, in response to Beth's tone, and watches as she strides about, unfolding tin foil from brisket; setting up yams, opening up rattatouille, etc. David may continue at his oat groats.)*

CANDI.   And then you just boil them an hour or so, just like that. And then when they're nice and soft, and your fork just goes in, then you just take them out and you put them in a pan. Then I just lay out a spoonful of sugar — just one spoonful for each yam. Of course if you've got brown sugar, or honey, that's best. Then you just pour on some orange juice — enough so they swim. Then you just pop 'em in the oven an hour or so, and that's it.

BRADLEY. I mean, with a cook like Tits, you know, that is it.

BARRY. Honey, don't you think you could try making Candi's yams?

BETH. *(Mad.)* What?

BARRY. Just a joke, honey.

CANDI. She's warming them. They're good like that.

BRADLEY. I like stuff heated like the second day —

CANDI. The tastes are like, there —

BRADLEY. And then it's easier for Candi to chew and shit.

BARRY. *(Opening refrigerator.)* Honey, have we got any of your casserole left?

DAVID. What casserole, Barry?

BARRY. Your sister's spinach.

DAVID. What?

BETH. *(Crossing back to refrigerator to get casserole.)* Dave, I don't know if you'd want to eat some of that. There's plenty left.

BARONE. It's got Cream of Mushroom soup in it.

BRADLEY. It comes from a can.

BARONE. *(Crossing to oven, turning it down.)* Doll, you've just set the oven too high. I know you're going to burn the yams.

CANDI. They get sweet like that. *(Beth drops the casserole, on purpose.)*

DAVID. Beth —

BARONE. For God's sake, Beth.

ARNOLD. Honey, maybe we just ought to go out and sit in the den.

CANDI. Let me help you with that.

BARONE. I'll get the paper towels, honey.

BETH. No, just leave it.

BRADLEY. Let's go out and smoke, Tits.

BARONE. Dave, you come with me.

DAVID. I'll stay with Beth.

BARONE. But, honey —

BETH. It's all right, Mom. He can just stay here.

BARONE. But, honey, what if she needs the burner from your oat groats?

BRADLEY. Let's go, Tits. *(Bradley and Candi exit to porch.)*

ARNOLD. Okay, Barone.

BETH. It's okay, Mom. I'm fine like this.

BARONE. I guess we can always eat the rattatouille cold. Like they do in France. *(Barone exits with Arnold.)*

BARRY. Beth, I'll just sit with your mom.

BETH. Fine, Barry.

BARRY. I'm right here. *(To David.)* Dave, don't forget what we talked about.

DAVID. Okay.

BARRY. She's your sister. *(He exits.)*

BETH. *(Alone with David.)* How are your oat groats doing?

DAVID. They're okay, I guess.

BETH. I mean, can you believe this? I mean, how I live? I mean, it's like Dad — like Dad just standing there and then ... I mean, can you help me out with this casserole?

DAVID. You know, Beth —

BETH. What? I mean, Mom coming in here, and Candi with her yams —

DAVID. I don't know, Beth, it's like —

BETH. Now what is it Barry wants you to say to me here?

DAVID. Well, it's like ...

BETH. Here, just hold the dust pan for me, here. *(As she's bending, sweeping.)* I mean, I just can't tell you how it's been with my back.

DAVID. I bet it's been bad.

BETH. It's just been the worst year of my life, I mean —

DAVID. I think it's just that everyone thinks —

BETH. You mean, Mom and Dad?

DAVID. And Barry —

BETH. Yeah — ?

DAVID. Well, just, if you lost a little weight, it might take some of the strain off your back.

BETH. "The strain off my back"! I can't believe you are saying this to me, Dave. "If I just lost a little weight ... " Do you think it's just that?

DAVID. No, of course I don't think that.

BETH. Did Barry say that?

DAVID. Look, every time I come home, I mean all I hear — it's like each second somebody can get me aside, every instant, they just keep saying to me, "Dave, you're the only one left. Talk to your sister about her weight —"

BETH. It's like I fell of a cliff.

DAVID. Yeah, well, now they're asking me to draw you back. *(A beat.)*

CANDI. *(Entering.)* Beth, I don't want to wear you out here. I just forgot in the rush of things to take out my beer. And then I just thought I'd better call Pammy to check on the kids. Can I use your phone, Beth?

BETH. Of course you can.

BARONE. *(Offstage. Calling.)* Doll — doll —

BETH. What is it?

BARONE. *(Entering with photo album.)* Doll, look what we found here.

BETH. What is it, Mom?

BARONE. Honey, it's the wedding pictures. The wedding pictures. Look at this one, David, here.

BARRY. *(Entering.)* Beth, how you doing in here?

BETH. I'm just warming the yams. *(She looks at Barone and David, then back at Barry.)* Who brought out the wedding album?

BARRY. Your Mom did, Beth.

BARONE. Oh, look at her, David, like that. *(To Beth.)* Oh, it makes me want to cry to see you like that.

BETH. Like what?

BARONE. Young and happy.

BETH. I am young and happy.

BARONE. It makes me want to cry, Beth.

BETH. Aaah gaad —

BARONE. You were such a beautiful baby. You were my bluebird of happiness. Don't you know how hellish it is, Beth, taking off the weight of babies?

BARRY. Where has the girl gone, Baroney, that I married?

BETH. *(Taking brisket and throwing it at Barry.)* Take your fucking brisket and get out of here.

BARRY. What?

DAVID. Beth —

BETH. Just take every goddamn bit of it and get out of here.

BARONE. *(Calling off.)* Arnie — Dad —

BETH. *(Pulling yams out of oven.)* Shit — it's hot —

BARONE. Don't burn yourself, Beth.

BETH. Just take every one of these yams. So god-damn easy to fix. Here — here are the yams — *(Beth begins throwing the yams one by one against the fridge, the kitchen counters, the walls....)*

BARONE. Don't burn yourself, Beth.

BETH. Here — eat these yams —

BRADLEY. *(Entering.)* What's happening, sweet ass?

BETH. *(Throwing the rattatouille at her mother.)* Here — you can stuff this rattatouille up your ass.

CANDI. My God, the yams!

BARONE. Beth, how could you? You were my bluebird of happiness ... Arnie — Arnie — Dad — Beth's throwing the yams.

ARNOLD. *(Offstage. Calling back.)* She's throwing the what?

BARONE. Beth's throwing the yams —

CANDI. Brad, I just think I need to go out for another cigarette.

BETH. I just want all of you to get out of here — all of you —

BARRY. Beth —

ARNOLD. *(He's entered.)* God damn it. Now I've got my boots in those yams.

BARONE. Let me see it, honey.

BRADLEY. *(Stopping her.)* Tits —

CANDI. You're right, Brad. What can I do, Beth, to help you clean up this mess?

BETH. I just can't stand it — not another minute of it. Just get out of here. *(A beat.)*

BARONE. *(Stepping into kitchen.)* Let me just get the paper towels out, honey. Your father got his boots in the yams.

BETH.   Damn it. I said, get the fuck out of here. Can't you hear me, Mom? Or are you too busy feeding me food and complaining I'm fat?

BARONE.   Doll, try this rattatouille. You'll never believe it: just peppers and eggplant.

BETH.   Mom!

BARONE.   Taste it, doll, off my dress.

CANDI.   *(Stepping up.)* Beth, let me help you with this mess.

BETH.   Oh, for God's sake, Candi, forget it. You don't give a shit. You must be so relieved we're not eating it.

CANDI.   Well, sometimes with the yams I can slurp down a bit ...

BETH.   Oh, for God's sake!

BARRY.   Brad, can I get you a drink?

BETH.   Oh, Barry, that's it.

BARRY.   What's it?

BETH.   Oh, Barry, for God's sake, do you think you can just wash everything down with a beer?

BRADLEY.   Sure, I could do a beer.

BETH.   I mean, do you think when you're standing there drinking, when you're eating the chocolate out of the refrigerator, when you're talking about me and my weight, or pulling boxes of Oreos out of the trashmasher, I mean, son of a bitch, Barry, don't you think I'm there?

BARRY.   Now this is my Beth, guys, God love her for the mouth on her.

BETH.   *(Screams.)* Aaaaaaaaaaaa — This is it!

DAVID.   *(Taking a moment, perhaps a deep breath, making a New Age gesture with his hands.)* Beth, quiet.

BETH.   Oh, right. We couldn't want your oat groats to get upset.

ARNOLD.   *(To Barone.)* Dolly, my god-damn boots are ruined by the yams.

BETH.   Okay, that's it. I'm getting the fuck out of here.

DAVID.   What? Where?

BETH.   Dave, if you like you can come with me. I'm getting out of here.

BARRY.   Honey, maybe when you go on your drive you could stop at Wolf's and pick us all up some ribs.

BETH.   Aaah gaaad, I am not getting ribs!

CANDI.   Dave, you can't eat ribs.

DAVID.   What?

CANDI.   Barbecued ribs. You can't eat that.

BARONE.   Remember, Dave, the years you would order the chili, and strawberry pie, while we all got ribs?

BETH.   *(Handing Dave his coat, pausing a moment.)* It's hard to believe, isn't it, Dave, that this is how I lived?

DAVID.   Let me just get my oat groats into a dish, and I'll go with you, Beth.

BARONE.   *(Bending down to pick up brisket.)* Maybe I can just wash off some of the brisket.

BARRY.   Dani Ann just did the floors.

BRADLEY.   I'll have that beer.

ARNOLD.   Beth, I just could use another cup of tea.

BETH.   Barry, you show him where it is.

BARRY.   What, honey?

BETH.   You show my Dad where the decaffeinated Earl Grey tea is. I'm getting the fuck out of here. *(Beth opens door to leave as Betty runs on from U. entrance.)*

BETTY.   *(Running on.)* Mommy — Mommy —

BETH.   What is it?

BETTY.   Mommy, I'm hungry.

BETH.   Oh, fuck, Dave. Fuck it. Fuck it. This existence!

DAVID.   What?

BETH.   Oh, fuck, Dave. I can't. I just can't.

DAVID.   Why not, Beth?

BETH.   I mean, fuck. Can you believe it: my life?! How can I walk out on it?

DAVID.   Beth ...

BETH.   I mean, fuck. You know, fuck it ...

BARONE.   *(After a beat, to David.)* Stay with me, dolly. I'll warm up the tofu here.

BARRY *(Turning on burner for tea kettle.)* You can use this burner, Arn.

ARNOLD.   That's fine.

BARRY. Baroney, why don't you call up Wolf's and see if you can order us some ribs?

BRADLEY. You know, we have got to be going, you know, for the kids.

BARONE. I'll look after your oat groats, dolly. Here, Beth, set them over here.

BETTY. Mommy ...

BETH. Just a second, honey.

BARONE. I'll just rinse off the brisket, and your father can slice it in the sink, Beth. *(A beat as music begins.)*

BETH. Can you believe it, Dave, that my life is this?

DAVID. I guess that's how it is.

BETH. Oh, yeah ... I mean, can you believe I just never got the fuck out of here?! *(A beat. Lights begin to fade, as voices overlap.)*

CANDI. *(On her knees, to Bradley.)* Well, can you believe that?

BRADLEY. You know, I just really can't.

BARRY. Arnie, who's ready for a drink?

ARNOLD. Just the tea for me, Bar.

CANDI. I mean, you know, well, it's her blood sugar level, I guess.

BRADLEY. That, and the size of her ass.

CANDI. The thing is, you know, she could use something sweet like these yams ... I mean, Dave: my life — this is it! *(A beat. Beth sighs. David puts his arm around her, hers is around Betty, as they stand looking out over lake.)*

BARONE. Honey, I'm just so heart-broken by all this. Now, what is the number at Wolf's?

ARNOLD. I don't know, dear. *(The tableau, set by the lights, of Beth, Betty, and David, looking out over lake. Candi on her knees cleaning up yams; Bradley drinking a beer. Arnold pouring the hot water over his tea bag; Barone dialing Wolf's, music ends as Blackout.)*

END OF ACT II

ENTR'ACTE II

David stands alone Onstage, spotlit.

DAVID.   Okay, so we ordered in barbecue finally. I'd forgotten, really, what a saga ribs from Wolf's could be. *(A beat.)* There was my father, with half a broiled chicken. My Mother pleading with Beth, "Try some cole slaw, honey." And telling me I could eat beans from her chili. "They're kidney beans, aren't they? Aren't they, honey?" And Candi, she got a rib caught in her back teeth. *(A beat.)* I remembered how, as a child, I'd had such indigestion. I thought, "Do I need this?" *(A beat.)* Then I left. I left with Brad and Candi. And, boy, I remembered how years before, really, I'd ride in the car with my brother, my Bradley; and we would smoke pot, and he would play music, and somehow — I don't know — that had just felt so free. *(A beat.)* So now there I was, squeezed to my knees in the backseat, Candi chain-smoking and sneezing; and Brad turning back continually to ask me, "So what the fuck's new in the Apple, New York, you know really?" *(A beat.)*

BLACKOUT

BRADLEY

ACT III

*Music at top. As music ends, lights up on Bradley standing
on the floor or seated on stereo speaker. David seated on the
floor, or on another speaker.*

BRADLEY. You know, when I went into the business with Dad,
I decided, I told him, "Look, Dad, if you want me here" — and
let's not forget this, that he asked me here ... He asked Candi
and me. He said, "Look, Brad, I want someone to come in
who can take over this thing for me, one day ..." So I reminded
him, I did, "Look, Dad; okay, we'll come here and we'll stay
here, maybe, and I'll go into the business with you, Dad, but
one thing, just one thing must be said." "What's that, Brad?"
he said. And I said, "If I'm coming here, Dad, you've gotta
know — I'm my own man. We are not joining the temple if
we don't want, not signing up for bar-mitzvahs, Dad ...
Look, Dad, the thing is this, I am coming here on my own,
with Candi — to make our own life, and our home; if I can't
go out and play music then I just can't. But I will be your
man 9:00 A.M. to 5:00 P.M. — or from 8:00 A.M. to — whatever — and then, you gotta understand, Carbondale or no
Carbondale, Dad, I am my own man." *(A beat.)*
DAVID. Yeah. And what did he say to that? *(A beat.)*
BRADLEY. I don't know. You know — one hit ... I'll just send
off my tapes and I'm out of here — out ... *(A pause. Bradley goes
to the cassette deck. Fiddles with the cassette player.)* Oh, fuck this
shit. Not this again. This fucking, fucking — mechanism.
That's what it is with life — all these fucking things ... Wait —
here it is. They get to you. Yeah ... *(Turning away from the deck.)*

You still don't smoke pot, huh?

DAVID. Naaa — I mean, I never did this dramatic thing of giving it up. I guess I just kind of forget that it exists.

BRADLEY. I know what you mean. Yeah ... I just got into it again. A little bit. I mean, I didn't for so long ... *(Back at the cassette deck. Discovers deck is not plugged into wall outlet.)* Wait — here it is. We're just dicking around here ... Here's the song. I wrote this — must have been, two years ago ... It seems so sad, remembering. *(A beat.)* I don't know ... You sure you don't get high, man? *(A beat.)*

DAVID. Yeah. So when did you start again?

BRADLEY. I don't know, man. *(A beat, finding the tape about at the right song.)* Here it is. Okay, David baby — listen. Fucking bit that I don't have a joint — well, we can pipe this ... You know, well, listen — I don't know ... Hang on, man. *(He walks to door. David sits up.)*

DAVID. Brad, what are you doing?

BRADLEY. Just for when I play the song, man. Not to wake the kids.

DAVID. Oh. You don't mean for the pot smoke?

BRADLEY. Naaaa. *(A beat.)* You know, sometimes I just feel so guilty, taking space for me. Like if I'm not doing something for her or the kids, I'm not like being a good daddy ...

DAVID. You feel that, Bradley?

BRADLEY. No. Just sometimes. Not really ... Shit ... *(He closes door. A beat.)*

DAVID. You know — it's great ... I mean, you know, even to think like in my life I could have to close the door on account of the kids ...

BRADLEY. Yeah. Shit ...

DAVID. I mean, sometimes I just think, how will I ever know what life is, how will I ever write about it, if I don't get married, and have children? Then I think, but oh, God, if I got married, had children, when would I ever have a minute to myself to write?

BRADLEY. I don't know, David — seems like you're living in New York doing all you ever wanted; there you are, writing all of your poems ... I always think, if I'd only trusted myself enough; myself and my music — Listen to this, man, it's good — I know it — one hit ... But then, Candi was pregnant, and I was out there in duck-fucking Colorado, driving my car with its trunk full of sweaters; these Bobbie Brooks outfits — you should have seen them, man — 'cause Dad, you know Dad, thought that was the way I'd learn to be responsible: "responsible" he said. So there I was, being a travelling salesman; and it was my birthday and I was alone, there ... Have you ever felt, David, so alone inside, you can't believe this is your life? I used to feel that, walking alone there at night ... I just remember, I got this joint then, from Candi — in a birthday card she sent me — and man, I smoked it, I was so happy. I wandered out under the starlight. There they were: the dippers, Cassiopeia ... And those cactus: like these thumbs stepping out against the sky, man ... And that starlight, so dazing, and distant ... And so, I invited her out and she stayed there — and somehow I found inside her the seeds of that starlight ... *(A loud crash from off.)* Now, what the fuck is that? Did you hear that?

CANDI. *(From off.)* Bradley!

BRADLEY. Candi's calling me — *(Yelling to her.)* What? *(Back to David.)* I just wish we could sit here and visit. *(Yelling back.)* Just a minute, honey. *(Back to David, to himself.)* One day, I'm going to have my own studio: here — like, air-proof; like no sound comes in ... It's like — I don't know — do you know what this is? I mean, there you are, with the chord, and the tune, or the theme — it's whatever — and Brian starts crying; you think, well, I'll get it later; and it's gone, man — gone forever ...

CANDI. *(Entering, as she does, turning up lights from wall dimmer.)* Brad — well, will you look at him?! Have you guys been smoking pot?

BRADLEY. What do you think, baby?

CANDI. Dave, would you like something to eat? I bet you would, huh? Now, what have I got that you eat? Would you eat some popcorn? I've got an airpopper. You don't have to use any oil in that —

BRADLEY. You know the type — like Dad has — that type.

DAVID. Yeah, maybe I'd have some ...

CANDI. *(About to exit.)* Brad, come look at Brian. He's running through the hallway with that sword again. He'll wake up Darcy —

BRADLEY. Okay, honey.

CANDI. *(Going.)* Brad —

BRADLEY. Okay — *(A beat, defeated. Then.)* Just one more hit. *(A pause. Crosses to wall switch and dims lights. Then, he takes the hit. Pontifical.)* So who is Brian, anyway? You know what I mean? It's like, sometimes you forget; you get so caught up in spanking, or scolding — whatever — you think he's just like you are — or he should be — you forget ... *(A beat.)* You have to hear this song, man.

CANDI. *(Entering, and turning up lights from wall switch.)* Here's some popcorn, David. Do you want salt on that or something?

DAVID. No, thank you.

CANDI. *(Starting to go.)* I'll make a bowl for us with salt, honey.

DAVID. Can you eat some of this? How are your teeth coming?

CANDI. Oh, it's coming.

BRADLEY. You know, she had to have seven root canals. Now they're afraid about her jaw.

CANDI. *(Exiting.)* I'll get us a salted bowl, honey.

BRADLEY. *(As she's gone.)* Maybe it'll never open again — I can't think that.

DAVID. What do you mean, never open?

BRADLEY. Well, if this surgery fails —

DAVID. What surgery?

BRADLEY. How can you talk without a mouth, man?

DAVID. What?

BRADLEY. It's like, what it is now is bone against bone. It's like there should be this Trident-like-gum sort of piece in her jaw, like over the bone, if you can imagine; there should be like gum you could kind of chew in the socket between where your jaws sort of meet. Now each time she chews, or bites on her teeth, she just clangs bone against bone ...

DAVID. Bradley, come on.

BRADLEY. Yeah, well now they're trying to force it back into place by this splint.

DAVID. And if that doesn't work, what?

BRADLEY. Well, if not, well, one day it'll just lock shut.

CANDI. *(Entering, with popcorn.)* Dave, have you got enough popcorn?

DAVID. *(Back to Candi.)* For now, yeah. Thank you.

CANDI. It's nothing to make more. I'm just afraid to start chewing. I am kind of hungry.

BRADLEY. It's a humdinger, yeah, but we'll get through it. The thing is, David, okay, this is physical pain; we can get through these things ... You just don't know what it is: the real Carbondale pain ...

DAVID. What do you mean?

BRADLEY. It's this Barry shit that's what gets to you ... That's what I mean ...

DAVID. Oh. How do you mean?

BRADLEY. Like he's the big man in the office — 'cause he was there before I was. He thinks he's the son like.

CANDI. Because he married your sister.

BRADLEY. I just don't like the man.

CANDI. He doesn't understand about my teeth like.

BRADLEY. Well, I finally realized I have spent my whole life looking over my shoulder for Mom and Dad; and I'm not going to spend the next thirty years looking over my shoulder for Barry. I just don't need that shit in my life anymore. *(A pause.)*

DAVID. But you must have other friends. You see other people?

CANDI. *(Lighting a cigarette.)* Sure we do — we have some ...

BRADLEY. Honest to God — there just aren't that many people in a town like this you can care about. Candi's kind of my best friend — and that's neat ... But I don't know ... Maybe it's our fault; we don't really branch out. But basically you know the types that are here, man ... I don't know — basically, we just don't have that many friends. It's kind of a shame, I guess, really. *(A pause.)*

DAVID.   But Mom and Dad take you out?

BRADLEY.   Can you imagine that, man? Mom won't leave us alone.

DAVID.   Tell me about it.

BRADLEY.   David, I live here. I have to deal with it.

CANDI.   Who has to deal with it? She tells me, I don't eat enough. "Honey, you don't chew, like ..." But everyone is different. You know like my Mom like just used to set out a Reese's cup and a Coke for me for breakfast. That's what I'm used to. That's what I like.

BRADLEY.   It's like, I'll get a call at work; they'll say, "Brad, it's your mom." I'll think, what have I done now like? I'll say, "Hello, Mom." Then she'll say to me, "Bradley, why can't Candi eat? Is it her teeth? Bradley, is she anorexic?" Can you imagine the fucking time we have spent? *(A beat.)* I don't know, man. It's like when I bought my Porsche. There I was. I saw it. I knew I could afford it. I really wanted it. Then why couldn't I buy it? It was goddamn fear of Dad. So you know what I did? I goddamn went out and bought it. And the next day I parked that red Porsche right next to him. There comes a time that you have to stand up and look the man in the eye and say, fuck you, that's who I am.

CANDI.   Maybe it's time, Brad.

BRADLEY.   Whether it's driving my Porsche, or playing my guitar in some goddamn Holiday Inn down in Henderson, or maybe just sticking my finger up my ass in public as Arnie Bader's son, that's just who I am. And you know, I think it's been good for Dad since I told him.

DAVID.   You told him that?

BRADLEY.   I think my just being here has been good for him. Just to let him see I'm my own man.

CANDI.   *(Biting into some popcorn.)* Ow —

BRADLEY.   What's that, baby?

CANDI.   Just my teeth. *(She stands.)* It'll just take a minute while I floss my teeth. *(Candi exits, Bradley goes to wall switch and dims lights.)*

DAVID.   Listen, Brad, why don't you just leave here?

BRADLEY.   What?

DAVID. Just leave here. There's nothing holding you. Take Candi with you and get out of here.

BRADLEY. What do you mean, man?

DAVID. Just fuck the salary. What about your dreams: Just take your Merrill Lynch account, and sell the house, and move out west. Buy yourself a ranch.

BRADLEY. Shit, I have thought about owning a ranch. What kind of life I would have. Just like raising horses, and writing music over grits ... And then, can you imagine what that might mean to a kid like say, Brian — to grow up like that, seeing mountains and shit? And then you just think, what with all the money they have, wouldn't you think that's the kind of life they'd really want their grand-kids to have? But then, well, that's Mom and Dad ... I mean, do you know this: when Candi called Mom to say she was pregnant? *(Calling to Candi.)* Honey, come in for this. Honey —

CANDI. *(Entering, perhaps with dental floss and another beer, turning up lights again.)* What's that, sugar?

BRADLEY. Mom, when you called her.

CANDI. When did I call her?

BRADLEY. To tell her of Darcy.

CANDI. You know what she said to me?

BRADLEY. You'll never believe what Mom said to her, man, when she called her to say she was pregnant. You'll never believe it. Candi, you tell him.

CANDI. She asked me, "Well, have you considered having an abortion?" *(A pause.)*

BRADLEY. Can you believe? That's the kind of thing you wouldn't even say to an animal, David. I mean, like if I had been dating a sheep or something ... Candi and I had already been married two years; we already had Brian ... I don't know, sometimes I just can't believe in my memory ...

DAVID. What do you mean?

BRADLEY. Like the stuff in it happened. *(A beat.)*

DAVID. Why don't you leave? Candi, why don't you and Brad just pack up your things and move away?

CANDI. Well, we do talk about these things ...

DAVID. Yeah. And what do you say?

BRADLEY. Man, the shit of it is —

CANDI. You just wouldn't believe.

DAVID. What is it?

BRADLEY. The oil market crash, man. I've got this debt at the bank like you wouldn't believe.

CANDI. It *is* hard to believe.

BRADLEY. And meanwhile I'm just living on my salary.

DAVID. It's pretty big.

BRADLEY. Yeah, but, David, when you've got a wife and kids — well of course, you wouldn't know about that — but when you do, man, money's not so easy.

CANDI. You've gotta have help.

BRADLEY. With her, with her teeth, she's gotta lay down, man. She can't just keep running all day.

CANDI. Sometimes when I sit it's just so painful and things.

BRADLEY. She's gotten so thin and things.

CANDI. It's just like I don't have enough weight on my bones to support me.

BRADLEY. Man, when you don't have weight on your ass, you just can't sit down comfortably.

DAVID. So what were you saying about money?

BRADLEY. David, we have just gotten accustomed to certain things ...

CANDI. When you live a certain way, with help and stuff, then you've gotten accustomed to spending a certain kind of money.

BRADLEY. You just can't believe. You have to keep buying. And then, man, if I want to play a gig, there's all the equipment and things. The thing is, I can't live any more off my salary ... We've got the mortgage here and things ...

CANDI. Your kids grow out of their clothes so quickly you can't believe.

BRADLEY. I just let him buy me in here. Now I can't afford to leave. *(A beat. David sits, or recedes, sad.)*

CANDI. David, aren't you hungry?

DAVID. Naaaa — *(A beat. Candi and Bradley exchange look about David.)*

BRADLEY. I'm working with a band now, Dave. It's lots of fun — it's neat. We'll meet here; Candi will lay out some dips or something. I mean, that girl goes all out — Jalopena bean dip — and guacamole, cheeses ...

CANDI. It's really so easy.

BRADLEY. And then we come in here and we jam for an hour. It's like finally there is like something that is mine.

CANDI. Is Chuck the one who really likes my nachos?

BRADLEY. Chuck really likes the bean dip and the nachos. We all just get into this shit. Then, the shit of it is, you know you've got to get up in the morning, act like you're working — 'Course, you wouldn't know about that ...

DAVID. Naaaa ...

BRADLEY. Shit. Well, you have got it good, man. It's not like you have to go fucking work in an office ... 'Course you should hear how Barry talks of you.

DAVID. How?

BRADLEY. He'll say — well ...

CANDI. Brad —

BRADLEY. He says like, about, well, that queer ...

DAVID. So that's what he says about me.

CANDI. He says worse than that.

DAVID. The thing is, Bradley, you know, I'm not gay. *(A beat.)*

BRADLEY. *(To Candi.)* Dave's not gay now, honey.

CANDI. Beats me. *(A beat.)*

DAVID. Well, I don't know. The thing is, for me, I can't think about myself or my sexuality without thinking about Rachel. Even when I was involved with Timothy, for all those years Rachel always remained first in my heart ... She knew that. She knows that ... I was just so afraid to make love to her. So of course she left me. She went to a party, and that's where she met Mary Ann ... So now they've gone off to Spain; and she writes me, they're happy together.

CANDI. Well, I just think that's great. I really do, Brad. Isn't that something?

BRADLEY. I'll say it's something. *(A beat.)*

CANDI. It must be nice to have no job and no kids, and just be free to go to Spain ...

BRADLEY. Yeah. Well, the thing is, you have got it easy, not having a family. You've got enough money.

71

CANDI.   The thing about money —

DAVID.   What?

CANDI.   You feel so bad taking it. I mean, here we are, jetting off to Dallas; then we saw that doctor in Galveston. Then there's that specialist up in Chicago your Mom heard of from her dentist in Florida — now, he's supposed to be excellent ... But meanwhile your Dad just keeps paying for all of it. And you think, maybe, maybe if you felt better for all this travelling, all this money, then maybe you'd think, okay, well, I am better. But it's like, I don't know; where is it going to end up? *(A beat.)*

BRADLEY.   Have we got some cocaine, baby?

CANDI.   There's that stuff Estelle left.

BRADLEY.   We can make numb lips. *(He locates the cocaine — in another box, or Candi exits to fetch it.)* You remember Estelle, don't you David, Candi's friend, the pharmacist at the wedding? She's just such a nice girl. We always think, if we could just find some nice guy for Estelle. You know, she's such a nice girl; she's so smart, she's got a good job — so what if she's got zits on her tits? So, there's more to who you are than what your face looks like.

CANDI.   *(Re-entering, if she's exited, with cocaine.)* Estelle has a problem of self-confidence.

BRADLEY.   Yeah. Let's set up some lines, man.

DAVID.   Not for me this time.

BRADLEY.   Now don't tell me this is like taking sugar, it's bad for your pancreas — whatever. You don't even eat this, man, it just goes up your nose like.

DAVID.   Oh, I see. What about when you make numb lips?

BRADLEY.   *(Setting up lines.)* I don't know, man.

CANDI.   *(Perhaps taking a dollar bill and starting to roll it, so it can be snuffed through.)* I don't know — it just gets so confusing. The specialist in Dallas, he tells you one thing. Then the guy in Memphis —

DAVID.   In Memphis?

BRADLEY.   We saw a guy in Memphis.

CANDI.   He like said if I just chewed on a splint and slept with the splint, the joint, it would all be all right.

BRADLEY.   Try a line of this, baby.

CANDI. I just want it on my lips, Brad.

BRADLEY. She likes to make numb lips.

CANDI. *(Taking cocaine onto her lips.)* And then — I don't know — the guy in Houston —

BRADLEY. *(Dabbing her lips.)* We saw a guy in Houston. He says like the splint will do nothing you'll waste time.

CANDI. *(Still taking cocaine onto her lips.)* And meanwhile your jaw is deteriorating —

BRADLEY. You know what, Candi baby? I should just play this song live for Dave.

CANDI. I would love that. Do I get to listen?

BRADLEY. *(Rising to exit.)* Sure. Just let me go get my instrument. *(Bradley exits.)*

CANDI. *(Alone on stage with David, turns to him.)* I just don't know what to eat sometimes. Like tonight — at dinner at Beth and Barry's ... I just can't eat sometimes when I'm not settled like. I just felt so uncomfortable, like everybody was looking to see what I'd eat. Barry was counting my beers, like.

BRADLEY. *(Re-enters, with his guitar.)* Here it is, guys.

CANDI. *(Rising.)* Excuse me a minute. I just have to fix one place where the cocaine's in my teeth. *(Pausing as she exits.)* Can I get you something to drink, Dave?

DAVID. No, no thank you. *(Candi exits. Perhaps Bradley plays a little tune and David dances; if not he just strums a warm-up chord, then.)*

BRADLEY. I think this song's going to be your type.

DAVID. I can't wait.

BRADLEY. *(Settling back in at the cocaine.)* You sure you don't want a line of this — ?

DAVID. Yeah.

BRADLEY. Huh?

DAVID. Yeah, I'm sure. *(A beat.)* You know, Brad, I was just thinking ... I mean, I can't get to where you are, Bradley. I can't get through my own thinking, and maybe just reach out my hand and say, "Bradley, don't do that cocaine ..."

BRADLEY. Yeah, I know what you mean ... The thing is, I don't do this so much as like I did before. *(He snorts a big line of cocaine.)* You know, when you've got a wife and kids, you've

73

got to be responsible. 'Course you wouldn't know about these things ...

CANDI.   *(Hurrying back in.)* Okay, here I am.

BRADLEY.   You want some lips? *(Candi shakes her head "no." Bradley stands.)* Now, okay, man, you'll hear about my life. *(He takes up the guitar, looks to Candi.)* I wrote this for us. *(He warms up a chord.)* Okay — here it is — ... *(Sings, accompanying himself on guitar.)*

"I just sit and feel alone sometimes
I do —

I feel there is no one who is mine
I do —

Then I think, you're waitin' for me
You hold out my baby toward me
I think, it's all right
And it's so fine
And it's so fine —

Sometimes I am in the office
Sittin' where the smoke and talk is
I think, I can't stand this job I do —
Yes, I do —

Then I know you're waitin' for me —
Sittin' home
With chicken for me
Cookin' on the stove, when day is through —

Yes, I do —

Oh, yes, I do —

We'll all sit and eat together
We won't talk about the weather
We'll all move into another room.
There we all can watch a movie too.

And that's the truth —

So, I think, if I'm alone there
You'll be there upon my shoulder
We can be alone together too — —
You and me and there's our baby too."

(A pause.) So what do you think, huh? I'm not sure about the ending.
DAVID.   I like it.
BRADLEY.   You do, Davey?
DAVID.   Yeah, it has your life in it, too.
BRADLEY.   They say the greatest art has life in it.
DAVID.   Yeah, it's true.
CANDI.   Well, I loved it.
BRADLEY.   Huh?
CANDI.   Don't you think, Dave, you could get him hooked up with someone?
BRADLEY.   A gig like someplace.
CANDI.   Don't you think if you took back that tape to New York you could play it for — I don't know who ...
BRADLEY.   I just think — one hit ...
CANDI.   I think it could be seen.
DAVID.   I could show it to some friends.
CANDI.   He just needs someone to listen.
BRADLEY.   Man, one hit! *(A loud crash from off.)*
CANDI.   Brian! *(A beat.)* I've gotta be heading for bed now, guys — with Brian.
DAVID.   It's so nice to see you again.
CANDI.   It really is. *(A beat.)* Brad, don't forget I've got that sofa being delivered tomorrow.
DAVID.   Where's that going?
CANDI.   Here, in this corner. Then I want something smaller — an arm chair — for over there ...
DAVID.   You've got furniture coming for in here?
CANDI.   We've got that armchair, and that sofa ...
BRADLEY.   You saw how she did the other rooms and shit, you knew she'd get in here.
DAVID.   But I thought this was your studio.
BRADLEY.   That's for later, man. I've just been playing in here.
DAVID.   But —

BRADLEY. I'm like going out to the garage.

CANDI. Which is better for the band.

BRADLEY. It's like, quieter out there.

CANDI. It's just more separate from the kids.

BRADLEY. There's just more room out there.

CANDI. We need a room to sit down and relax.

BRADLEY. She's got like no weight left on her ass. *(A beat.)*

DAVID. *(Giving in.)* So, you've got an armchair coming, and that divan ...

CANDI. Yeah, that sofa for in here. Then I've got this bar made out of bone we bought in New Mexico.

DAVID. After you saw the doctor?

BRADLEY. An oral surgeon there.

CANDI. Yeah. It's just made out of bone. I want it over here. Then I found this shell painting floor lamp. I mean, it's got shells for the shade ... And it just casts a light like, you know, in my Mom's house ... That kind of light we used to have and things ... I mean, my Mom would just come out at Christmas; and we would like all just have Kool Aid ... I mean, you remember Kool Aid, don't you, Dave ...? I mean, now I just think with that floor lamp, we can entertain ...

BRADLEY. She's got such a talent, David. One day I'm going to set her up in her own little shop, just do designing of other guys' houses ...

CANDI. It's really so easy.

BRADLEY. Give me a kiss, hon. *(Bradley kisses Candi good-night, careful not to injure her jaw.)*

CANDI. I'll see you tomorrow, Dave. When we wake up we can talk about how we could fix up your apartment.

DAVID. My apartment?

CANDI. Maybe when I come up to see your dentist Mike about my teeth, I can look at the size of it. Just for talking's sake.

DAVID. That'd be great.

CANDI. *(Exiting.)* Good-night, guys. *(A beat.)* Now, don't make too much noise and wake Brian.

BRADLEY. Okay, hon.

CANDI. And no frying shrimp, huh? Unless you wake me. I always get the munchies, after my numb lips ... *(She exits. Then, we hear a loud crash.)*

BRADLEY. *(Going to check out the crash.)* Can you believe it?

DAVID. Yeah ...

BRADLEY. Hang on, man. *(He closes door. Goes to wall switch and dims lights, then.)* Now let's just settle back in where we were, man. You tell me about you, and Rachel, and your life, and things ...

DAVID. Yeah, well, it's really amazing, I mean, you know, how much my life has changed.

BRADLEY. Huh ...

DAVID. I mean, do you feel that, Bradley, like your life has changed?

BRADLEY. Well, yeah; I mean, you know, it's fucking changed ... I mean, like, you know, — can you believe it? — all of these things ...? *(A beat.)* But then like, you know, it's like, I don't know, you know, it's like, shit, I don't know, the same ...

DAVID. Yeah.

BRADLEY. Here you go, Davey, just toot up one line with me here, like the way we just did ...

DAVID. Not just yet.

BRADLEY. I mean, fuck, you remember the number of spoonfuls we did ...? I mean, Dave, you were my best man.

DAVID. Oh, yeah ... And now here I am. And here you are ...

BRADLEY. Oh, yeah ...

DAVID. I mean, you know, really, after all those years we were kids, I mean, when did we start really ever being like friends ... ? I mean, it didn't start, really, did it, Bradley, until I would come home from college —

BRADLEY. And I'd get a lid.

DAVID. Oh, yeah ... It was when we would sit —

BRADLEY. Doing a dooby —

DAVID. Oh, yeah ...

BRADLEY. Remember ...

DAVID. We'd wander out into the back yard together; and you'd name the stars to me, their mute constellations ...

BRADLEY. I was taking astronomy then.

DAVID. Uhuh, yeah ... And I just felt so protected ... Like this was a place — I mean, under your arm — I could just stand still and be silent, and know I lived ... I mean, like, it was okay for me to be quiet: just Davey, the quiet kid again ... And nobody in the world could make fun of me, Bradley, because you would be there to love me the way you did ...

BRADLEY.   Well, you know, Dave, I did ...

DAVID.   I know, Bradley.

BRADLEY.   I did ...

DAVID.   *(After a beat.)*   And then, oh, Bradley, don't you remember, when we would come in —

BRADLEY.   And fry up shrimp —

DAVID.   Oh, yeah ... And then, when we'd talk, it was all of our dreams, Brad: how we were going to get out of here — how we would live ...

BRADLEY.   Huh ... Yeah ...

DAVID.   Then you'd move to the piano, Bradley; and you'd just sit there: banging out song after song you'd just written; and, Bradley, I would just dance ... Even in a backbrace, Bradley, I would just dance ... I'd feel your music like something inside me; like there was some kind of hope for the life I would live ... Like after all that back accident I could still dance ...

BRADLEY.   I could make you feel that?

DAVID.   Oh, Bradley, you don't know what it meant, to see you sitting there, smiling and laughing; like you were playing a love song for me while I danced ...

BRADLEY.   Oh, Davey. My man ...

DAVID.   And now I come home, and where is the dancing, Brad?

BRADLEY.   Man, I can't play the piano like now with the kids.

DAVID.   Oh, I know that. No, I was just remembering, a minute ...

BRADLEY.   Here, do one spoon with me, man ...

DAVID.   Shit! *(He gets up, moves away.)*

BRADLEY.   I mean, you just don't know how it is ... I mean, this is like something like, well — you just won't tell this to Mom and Dad?

DAVID.   What do you think, Brad?

BRADLEY.   I mean, just all we need is more of Barry coming

here and breathing down our necks.

DAVID. What is it, Brad?

BRADLEY. I mean, well, you'd never believe ... But she's gotten into doing pretty heavy Perkodan.

DAVID. Perkodan?

BRADLEY. Perkodan for pain, man. I mean, she's got prescriptions all over for this shit. From Estelle you know she gets it. Then she keeps getting it from one guy in Florida. Then there's the guy we saw in Kansas City; the guy in Memphis, then the guy in Houston, and all that ... I mean, you just have to wonder, man, when will it end? How will she ever come back from the Perkodan? *(A beat.)* I mean, David, do you know what it is, to be feeding your kids and afraid that your wife'll drop dead ... ? I mean, she goes days and days without eating, man ...

DAVID. Oh, yeah. *(A beat.)* But what is left of your life, Brad? What is left of that?

BRADLEY. *(After a beat.)* Man, you don't know how it is. *(A beat.)* I mean, this is Carbondale, man. I mean, really, the people you see here! I mean, you just have to wonder, what can these people even be living for, man? I mean, what am I living for? Am I just one of them? I mean, you just see me — I'm one of them — the zombies — mowing down the aisles of Appleman's — just munching like on peanut M & M's. And I mean, then are we just going to die; and then will we have ever lived?

DAVID. Wake up Brad. I mean you just sit here, complaining, complaining: about Barry, about Mom and Dad ...

BRADLEY. Well, fuck, you don't live here and have to deal with it, man.

DAVID. So get out of here, Brad.

BRADLEY. Yeah, well, that's easy to say, man.

DAVID. But, Brad, I got out of here. I didn't have more; I had much less money when I left than you now have.

BRADLEY. David, you're a single man.

DAVID. Yes, but, Bradley, that's the thing you have. The joy you have ... I mean, Brad, you have a wife who loves you. You have two kids ... I mean, Brad, you have enough money ... I mean, maybe you can be happy, just living here ...

BRADLEY. Maybe I can.

DAVID. Or maybe you could be happier just picking up, heading out to a ranch ...

BRADLEY. Fucking maybe it's that ...

DAVID. But I mean, Brad, you could go try that. I mean, for three months, just renting a ranch ...

BRADLEY. Well, yeah, I hadn't thought of that.

DAVID. Or I mean, you could just bring Candi and the kids, and come live with me for three months in New York. I could take out your tape. I do have some friends ...

BRADLEY. Now I'd go for that ...

DAVID. The thing is, Bradley, whether it's staying here, or getting a ranch, or just getting a hit, I mean, Brad, you have got so much. You have got it all, Brad. *(A beat.)* You only have to stand up again. *(A beat.)* I mean, I don't know, Bradley; you can't just keep sitting here so sad ... *(A long beat.)*

BRADLEY. *(Offers David his hand; as David takes it, Bradley stands.)* You have fucking got it, man. *(A beat. As he stood up, he's spilt the cocaine.)* Oh, shit!

DAVID. What's that?

BRADLEY. Fucking shit!

DAVID. Brad, what is it?

BRADLEY. The cocaine, man. I spilt it.

DAVID. Forget it.

BRADLEY. "Forget it"? Fucking shit. I mean, this was cocaine. Do you know what that is?

DAVID. Yeah, I know what it is.

BRADLEY. You know what this cost me, this shit? David, this cost me 400 dollars.

DAVID. What is the cost of your life, Brad? What is the measure of that?

BRADLEY. Oh, David, David, fucking shit ... I mean, David, I was listening. But, this was cocaine.

DAVID. Bradley, why do you think I came home? Why do you think I'm here? *(A beat.)* I mean, I don't know what all it is ... But I'm just so scared myself too of losing you, Brad.

BRADLEY. *(After a beat.)* C'mon, man. *(A long beat.)*

DAVID. I'll never give up on you, Brad. *(A long beat.)*

BRADLEY. You're my man. *(A long beat.)* The thing is, you just don't know the shit with this carpet. How Mom got so involved with this ... Candi wanted carpet like this — it's all wool, you know, man — and Mom said, how can you consider spending money on carpet like that; you don't know how it is with growing kids.

DAVID. I can just imagine.

BRADLEY. The nice thing about wool, and we didn't even bother to answer her this, is it all just comes right up from the carpet — *(Bradley bends over and snorts cocaine up from carpet.)*

DAVID. I can't believe this.

BRADLEY. *(Continuing to sniff it up.)* Like let's just say like if Brian spills orange juice, or say like Darcy starts coughing and vomits down here, it just like beads up, like it does on a sweater ...

DAVID. Oh, God, Brad.

BRADLEY. We really are starting to get into natural things. *(A beat, he fingers up the last cocaine.)* Now why don't we just roll up one last little doobie? I'll just roll off what's on the seeds, man. And listen, if you don't want to smoke it, that's fine by me, man. And then let's go out like we just used to do, and look up at the stars again ... *(Music begins softly.)*

DAVID. *(After a beat, a decision.)* I could do that. *(A beat.)*

BRADLEY. I don't know, man. It's like sometimes you think, you know —

DAVID. What?

BRADLEY. You just feel like —

DAVID. Brad, what?

BRADLEY. I don't know — nothing. No. *(A beat, tableau as the brothers come together.)* Let's just go look at the stars, man. They're still there. *(Music ends as Blackout.)*

END OF ACT III

EPILOGUE

David stands alone Onstage, spotlit.

DAVID.   So that was it. What could I say to Bradley? We looked at the stars. I thought, "God, it's just starting. How much is left if tomorrow's Thanksgiving?"   *(A long beat.)*

BLACKOUT

THE END

EPILOGUE

PROPERTY LIST

ACT I/ARNOLD

OFFSTAGE LEFT:
> Dial phone
> Lipstick – Barone's Fix-Up Kit
> Mirror – Barone's Fix-Up Kit
> Comb – Barone's Fix-Up Kit
> Diamond pin (Barone)
> Blue pant suit (Barone)
> 2 dresses, 1 pink (Barone)

OFFSTAGE RIGHT:
> Cole slaw in bowl
> Peanut butter sandwich on plate
> Watermelon on plate
> Glass of water
> Fork
> Napkin
> Serving tray

ON STAGE:
> Table cloth
> Clock
> Flower arrangement
> Golf club (Arnold)

ACT II/BETH

ON STAGE:
> Oreos
> Tea in box (2 bags)
> White chocolate in white box
> Beth's purse and keys
> Spinach casserole
> Serving spoon
> Table spoon

Can opener
Tea cup
Phone
Strainer
Sauce pan
Bowl
Tea kettle
Roll of paper towels
Dish towel
Sponge
Dustpan and small whisk broom
Ash tray

PROP TABLE:
Pineapple
Barone's bag with flash camera
Cornbread in pan
Rattatouille in casserole pan (unbreakable)
Beef brisket in roasting pan
Candi's bag with cigarettes, lipstick, lighter
Yams in pan
Six pack Amstel Light/two filled with water
and recapped
Ice tea (for refill)
Photo album
Ice tea glass with fake ice cubes
Coffee cup/water
Small basket with yellow feathered chicken
costume, needle and thread
Suit case containing
Pressure cooker
Wooden spoon
Strainer

ACT III/BRADLEY

ON STAGE:

   Cocaine in small paper envelope (powdered sugar)
   Baggie with pot seeds (cat nip)
   Packed pot pipe (tobacco)
   Tin for marijuana
   Rolling paper
   Lighter
   Dollar bill (Candi)

PROP TABLE:

   4 Amstel Lights/filled with water
   2 bowls popcorn (1 medium and 1 small)
   Lighter
   Cigarettes
   Compact containing
      Razor
      Small cocaine envelope (powdered sugar)
      Cocaine Straw
   Pillow
   Crash box
   Serving tray
   Dental floss (optional) (Candi)
   Guitar (Bradley)

COSTUME PLOT

ACT I/ARNOLD

Barone: Pink robe, pink slippers, blue silk pant suit, pink dress, diamond pin, dress shoes

Arnold: Grey slacks and black belt, blue cardigan sweater, light blue dress shirt, casual shoes

ACT II/BETH

Barone: Paisley skirt, magenta blouse, dress shoes

Arnold: Maroon cordurory pants and brown belt, tan shirt, off-white sweater, cowboy boots

Beth: Fat suit, pink sweatsuit, tennis shoes

Barry: Bath towel, blue Lacoste polo shirt, tan pants, brown shoes

Betty: Pink towel, pink sweat suit or pajamas

Brad: Light plaid shirt, blue jeans, cowboy boots

David: Tweed jacket, black turtleneck, black pants and belt, black shoes

Candi: Purple blouse, suede skirt, casual pumps

ACT II/BRADLEY

Brad: Light plaid shirt, blue jeans, cowboy boots

David: Black turtle neck, black pants and belt, black shoes

Candi: Kimono or robe, white chemy top, yellow silk
               pants, slippers

"Bradley Song"

"Bradle/s song"

NEW
PLAYS

APOCALYPTIC BUTTERFLIES
ANCIENT HISTORY
BEEN TAKEN
A FLEA IN HER EAR
THE HEART OUTRIGHT
FOG ON THE MOUNTAIN
MR. WILLIAMS AND MISS WOOD
OATMEAL AND KISSES
PVT. WARS (Full Length)
TO CULEBRA
REASONABLE CIRCULATION
ASCENSION DAY
THE DOCTOR WILL SEE YOU, NOW
THE LAST GOOD MOMENT OF LILY BAKER

Write for information as to
availability
DRAMATISTS PLAY SERVICE, Inc.
440 Park Avenue South   **New York, N.Y. 10016**

CARNAL KNOWLEDGE
THE LOMAN FAMILY PICNIC
THE MOONSHOT TAPE
A POSTER OF THE COSMOS